ISBN 978-1-330-50030-9
PIBN 10070264

This book is a reproduction of an important historical work. Forgotten Books uses state-of-the-art technology to digitally reconstruct the work, preserving the original format whilst repairing imperfections present in the aged copy. In rare cases, an imperfection in the original, such as a blemish or missing page, may be replicated in our edition. We do, however, repair the vast majority of imperfections successfully; any imperfections that remain are intentionally left to preserve the state of such historical works.

1 MONTH OF
FREE
READING

at

www.ForgottenBooks.com

By purchasing this book you are
eligible for one month membership to
ForgottenBooks.com, giving you
unlimited access to our entire
collection of over 700,000 titles via
our web site and mobile apps.

To claim your free month visit:

www.forgottenbooks.com/free70264

English
Français
Deutsche
Italiano
Español
Português

www.forgottenbooks.com

Mythology Photography **Fiction**
Fishing Christianity **Art** Cooking
Essays Buddhism Freemasonry
Medicine **Biology** Music **Ancient
Egypt** Evolution Carpentry Physics
Dance Geology **Mathematics** Fitness
Shakespeare **Folklore** Yoga Marketing
Confidence Immortality Biographies
Poetry **Psychology** Witchcraft
Electronics Chemistry History **Law**
Accounting **Philosophy** Anthropology
Alchemy Drama Quantum Mechanics
Atheism Sexual Health **Ancient History**
Entrepreneurship Languages Sport
Paleontology Needlework Islam
Metaphysics Investment Archaeology
Parenting Statistics Criminology
Motivational

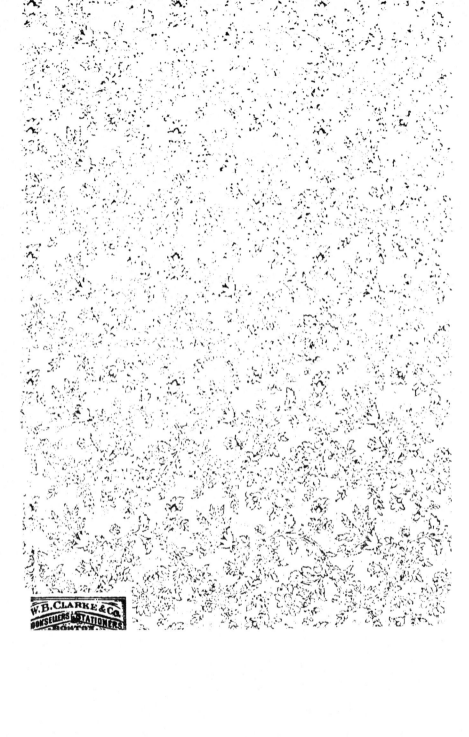

CHARLES ELLIOTT PERKINS.

THE GEORGIAN BAY

AN ACCOUNT

OF

ITS POSITION, INHABITANTS, MINERAL INTERESTS, FISH,
TIMBER AND OTHER RESOURCES,

WITH

MAP AND ILLUSTRATIONS.

PAPERS READ BEFORE THE CANADIAN INSTITUTE

BY

JAMES CLELAND HAMILTON, M.A., LL.B.,

CHAIRMAN OF THE HISTORICAL SECTION,

Author of "The Prairie Province."

TORONTO :

JAMES BAIN & SON.

1893.

E. MARLBROUGH & Co.,   CHAS. SCRIBNER'S SONS,
London, E.   New York.
TICKNOR & Co.,
Boston.

Entered according to Act of the Parliament of Canada, in the year One thousand
eight hundred and ninety-three, by JAMES CLELAND HAMILTON, in the office
of the Minister of Agriculture.

TO'

THE CREW OF THE "WHITE SQUALL"

AND

TO ALL THE JOLLY FISHERMEN

WHOSE NETS ARE CAST 'MONG THE ISLES OF

THE GEORGIAN BAY.

Rosedale, Toronto,
May, 1893. ·

ERRATA.

Page 148—Read ; The total area of Hudson Bay, of which James Bay is part, is 397,000 square miles.

Page 166—Aurora Borealis. Read ; *nimi-i-diwag.*

Page 168--Parry Sound ; *Wah-sah-ko-sing,* meaning Driftwood all around the shore.

The photograph of Champlain's astrolabe is from the original, through the courtesy of R. S. Cassels, Esq. The other illustrations are from original pencil sketches made by Mrs. Jameson during her "Summer Rambles" of 1837, in possession of Mr. Robert Bain, who has kindly permitted their reproduction in this volume.

" And this our life, exempt from public haunt,
  Finds tongues in trees, books in the running brooks,
  Sermons in stones, and good in everything."

CONTENTS.

CHAPTER I.

CHAPTER II.

CHAPTER III.

CHAPTER VI.

CHAPTER VII.

CHAPTER VIII.

The Skipper, an accomplished, though amateur sailor, had his compass and box of government charts of these waters as prepared from survey by Commanders Bayfield and Boulton, R.N. This is the vessel we were in, usually called a Macinac. She was 32 feet from stem to stern, 8 feet 4 inches beam, her fo'castle was 10 feet 6 inches, and a small locker was also at the stern, which was pointed as the bow. The two masts carried six hundred feet of canvas. Large stones and wooden railway ties formed the ballast. A tent, oval in shape, 7 feet 6 inches by 10 feet, lay rolled up ready to be raised as night fell, and fastened with hooks to the deck. A sixteen foot skiff was towed behind as a dingy. The Dominion flag flew from the peak of the mainsail. The craft had been used as a fishing smack, but was cleaned and refitted, under our good Skipper's direction, for this trip. We were seven, but one waited till the port of Parry Harbour was reached and there joined the party. For personal comfort, each had his valise and bag of blankets. Alfred the Steward had charge of the provisions; and well filled boxes under the fore-deck attested his assiduity. To the Skipper we owed much for brilliant foresight; 25 yards of cotton at five cents a yard, made into narrow cases and filled with hay, formed comfortable mattresses at night and, during the day, were stowed in the fo'castle, or used as seats. Old and warm clothing was in order. 'Misery' had his guitar, 'Ninety' had his little flutes in three keys. We started on an even keel, with even tempers, and dull care and Colpoy's Bay were soon left far behind.

The sails are full; wharfs, pretty villas and farms are past. High limestone cliffs rise up in the west; Cape Croker is in view, and we sheer off eastward, past Hay Island. The open is soon reached. As night comes on, the lights of Owen Sound and Cape Rich are seen, but the course is through the centre of the big Bay and with the Christian Islands far on our starboard.

The wind for a time blows a gale and double reefs are taken in the sails; still on she goes with us all up on the weather gunwale, and the water giving an occasional dash over the coamings as she heels over to the freshening gale. This lasted for a couple of hours, then a calm fell, and we almost drifted and got some sleep, with a lantern hung out. When the sun rose, we were pretty seedy, but a cup of coffee, concocted over the coal-oil stove, steadied our nerves and a good breeze generally bore us along till we came to the Red Rock lighthouse, where we hailed a fishing smack and asked for the course to Parry Sound. "If you will haul up a bit I'll go with you," answered a young fisherman. Glad of his company, we soon had Adam Brown on board and in charge of the tiller. A jolly fisher was he ; every rock in the bay and each short cut, through the mazes of the islands, was familiar to him. We were tied up in Parry Harbour as the sun set. Here we had our first supper, using a vacant shed for dining room. Some rested on board, others in the shed, and all slept soundly and awoke ready for our bath and breakfast. Then we went up through the village, had

a fine view from the hotel site—a beautiful spot set
high over the bay—waited till some showers passed
and, with Adam and sunshine, were off for the Minks
soon after noon. We stopped an hour at Kill-bear
Point, and, after a fine sail, got to the Minks about 9
p.m. The fishermen welcomed us heartily and gave us
the use of a shanty, where supper was soon spread. We
were invited to the gaieties going on near by, where
appeared a house full of a merry party. A visiting
fiddler made music, and shoes, not the lightest, beat
the floor, not the smoothest, and happy couples performed, as they were called, cotillions, quadrilles and
Sir Roger. 'Misery,' our amiable musician, brought
his guitar, and all went merry as a marriage bell.

"Take your places," "First couple advance," "Prom-
enade all," were some of the orders of the young fisherman, with broad weather-beaten face, full of enjoy-
ment, who acted as dance master. The guitar's sweet
tones aided the fiddler. Little ones dozed in the arms
of their smiling mothers, sitting on hard benches, and
the rugged features of the men relaxed as they looked
on. Such fun had not been at the Minks for many a
night. All was laughter and music and hammering
of feet. It was a strange contrast to the quiet scene
before us, as we passed the open door. Waves splashed
and sparkled in moonlight so clear that we could see
the roses and hyacinths that sprung from crevices in
the rocks. Orion was up in the east. The Aurora
flashed and danced to and fro in the north-west horizon, and the red shield of Mars, nearer to us that night

than he would be for many a year, held guard over the south.

All aboard again, a young fisherman took the helm, the breeze caught the sails, a quick run was made across a little bay, then a tack was taken, the painter thrown out and our vessel was run up on a shelving rocky shore. A vacant cabin was given us, where we were soon settled, and in bunks, for what remained of the night.

In the morning we found the Minks to consist of a number of rocky islands, on parts of which was sufficient soil to sustain grass, bushes and flowers, among which were the single pink rose, violet and strawberry, red raspberry and whortleberry plants. A solitary cow roamed through the bushes. Next morning we arose late, had breakfast, some fished ; a party took the ' White Squall ' and sailed to Franklin island. They got back at 9 p.m., without game, but had seen some ducks and partridges, an eagle on a high pine, and a rattlesnake. A fisherman brought in a snake, which looked like the Fox-snakes in the Canadian Institute collection. He called it a Copperhead. It was five feet long, and swam towards his boat holding up its head, when he shot it. In the evening, some of the young men came and joined our camp. They were intelligent and pleasant companions. One of them had fished off the Orkneys, but most of those at this station were Canadians from Collingwood, Meaford or Owen Sound. All were excellent sailors and could, without a chart, steer their boats on the shortest

course through the mazy channels of the Bay. The
arms of some were tatooed, sailor fashion, with boats
or anchors. Their songs were of the salt water:
'Tom Brown,' ' Charley Taylor, Ruler of the Sea,'
' The Three Brothers, a sad tale of the Spanish Main.'
Their management of the vessels was interesting.
They moved, among the islands and over shoals, as a
bicycle on the asphalt. Flocks of gulls, grey and
white, and of the smaller red-legged species, here
called " garnets," flew about or rested tamely on the
rocks ; when the fish are cleaned, they come and
greedily devour the offal, here thrown away, but at
other stations utilized for the oil which it yields.

The weather was windy, so that the men did not
go to their nets, nor were we successful with our
lines. We took the dingy and went from one to another of the Minks islands, throwing our hooks into
the pools. Our want of success was to some. extent,
perhaps, due to the fact that the watchful fishermen,
when they find a pool full of fins, haul a seine in it
and secure even the bass and pickerel. They never
use a rod, but sometimes throw a troll. We walked
about and picked flowers on the parts of the islands
covered with verdure. Wild roses and hyacinths, or
blue bells, and violets were common, and of fruits, the
raspberry, whortleberry, a dark currant and small
gooseberry, haws, bil-berries and pin-cherries were
ripe, and there were many vines of the strawberry,
pigeon-berry and wintergreen. " Is your fishing off
the Orkneys like that here ?" we asked of the young

Orkney man. "Oh, no," he said ; "here we sometimes have a little rough and foggy weather, but the men know how to manage and don't often get into danger. The nets may have to be out a few days longer than we wish, but off the Orkneys we go in rather bigger vessels, set our nets for the herring, and then, as the tide goes out, we must stay by and follow them, rain or shine, haul and bring them in, as the tide turns and comes with us.   Here we fasten the nets to an-chored floating buoys and leave them, until we have good weather to go out to them, from five to fifteen, or even twenty miles away, as the weather permits. The nets go down to the bottom, ten to forty fathoms, but when so far down it is hard work hauling them.". There were no steam craft used here, but the vessels of some of the men, notably the Messrs. Farr, were rigged with top-sail and jib and fitted up almost as yachts. Their centre-boards were of wood and were found safer and easier to manage than if of iron. These vessels were all pointed, fore and aft, like our own, and none more than 35 feet long ; while the crafts of Lake Huron fishermen which we met were almost invariably square in the stern, but of a like tonnage. Some of them were of "partridge build," the prow sharp and rising gracefully above the water.

On Saturday p.m. we steered away with a good wind, took the outer channel northward, passed the lights of Point au Baril and Byng Inlet, made more than fifty knots, with scarce a tack, until we neared the light off the Bustards. It was dark, so we did not venture through the shorter but intricate channel, but went round the rocky reef to the west and tied up opposite the wharf of Yankee island, had supper and slept on board.   Next day we visited French River, three miles across the Bay, a great lumber centre, with two mills, immense piles of pine boards, and long elevated tramways for the removing and hauling of the lumber.   We returned to the Bustards, tying up at 'Highland Home,' another island.   Here were many shanties but most of the fishermen were gone, as the season was waning.   Some of them were from Lake Huron and will fish there in October. One of them said that he and his partner had taken 25 tons of fish this season.   He was unusually fortunate, from 8 to 10 tons were as much as most of those here admitted to have secured.   They got $70 a ton from the Buffalo Fish Company, whose agent is here.   As the smacks come in from the grounds they are un-loaded, the fish dressed by removal of their entrails, weighed, and then packed in ice in the waggons, or boxes set on wheels, ready to be removed, as each box is filled, on the tugs—'The Clark' or 'The Jones.' Each box contains 1200 pounds of fish.   Here, too, "the barbarous people showed us no little kindness." We used a shanty for dining-room and had good company and music from the active young agent in charge of the store, and others.   We left the Bus-tards on Tuesday morning, had a good run on a westerly course, landed for dinner on a rocky island which rises very bold and large out of the water.

It was the resort of innumerable gulls that rose, screaming, as we approached. The top of the rock gave an excellent view of the surrounding bay and of the shore lying to our north, with rocks and islands innumerable stretching into the misty distance. This region has not yet been surveyed or fully delineated on the government charts, and it is hoped that Commander Boulton will be permitted to complete his admirable work, so invaluable to all navigators of these waters.

We arrived at Killarney at 11 p.m., in rain, and tied up at a wharf. Three of us went to the Algoma Hotel, the others had the more room for comfort on board, under cover of tent and sails. Next morning the interesting village was seen. Three large steamers came in on their way to or from the Soo'. Many Indians were strolling about, dressed as white folk, all comfortable and happy in appearance. They were from the Reserve on Manitoulin Island, called Wikwemikong. I conversed with two of them, Tom Salter, or Skeabunk, and Edward Selko, and found that the language of the Missisaugas, of Scugog, as given in the thesis of Dr. A. F. Chamberlain, of Clark University, was well understood by them. They are mostly Chippewas. Several Macinacs were at the wharf, owned by Indians and used in fishing. Now they carried squaws and papooses and bushels of whortleberries, picked by them. The young squaws were bartering on the wharf, stout old dames held the babies and kept order in the vessels among the little

red folk and their dogs.   There are many half breeds
at Killarney, mostly French and Roman Catholic, and
there is a small Roman Catholic church.   Killarney is
at the eastern termination of a rich mineral region, as
yet little developed, but very interesting to geologists.
The scraping of the ice, as the great bergs ground
slowly along in a remote age, from the north-west to
the south-east, is distinctly visible on the flat rocks
in the steamboat channel. The formation is Huronian.
The nickel deposits, now worked with much profit,
are in the Sudbury district, north of Killarney, and
will be further referred to. (a)

Leaving Killarney, we made sail along the coast
easterly a few miles and entered a pretty cove. Here
we anchored; some fished and others wandered over the
land with guns for awhile.   The moss, covering rocks
and stumps, here and elsewhere on this shore, was deep
and yielding to the touch, and in hue, rich and varied,
from soft sea-green to heathery purple.   As the sun
shone on its dewy spires, they glistened like gems.

With wind astern, we next struck south for Squaw
island, going for a time with sails 'wing-a-wing.'
Many islands were passed, rocky and barren, but
Green island appeared to our left as an oasis clad with
verdure of trees, shrubs and flowers. We entered
Squaw Island harbour, in shape a horse-shoe, 500
yards across. The houses, the usual summer shanties, are on the south side. As our boat passed in, a
score of men and boys came to meet us. We ran

(a) See Chapter III.

upon a stony neck of land to the east and proceeded to prepare for supper. The fishing begins at the end of April and ends about the middle of August. There had been forty-seven smacks and three tugs employed here. Twenty-seven of the vessels had left. There were many nets on reels and spread on the rocks. Men were unrolling them, women and children were about the houses, all looking happy and comfortable. The island is of limestone, two miles long and half as wide. A light soil has formed over part of the rock, and this is covered with low cedars, spruce, balsam and juniper bushes. Among these may be found some wild fruit. The people are from various parts of the Bay, Collingwood, Lion's Head, Meaford and Killarney. Though of diverse creeds, all here, including a good Chippewa, joined in building a Mission Church, of which the missionary was architect and chief carpenter. The women do not work at the fishing or nets. The children go to a school conducted by Mr. Menzies, the excellent young Presbyterian missionary stationed here for the summer.

August 11th. Dashed out of the heel of the horseshoe, with a spanking breeze on a south-west course. Grand Manitoulin was before our prow, with Cape Smith on its north-east, and the Killarney and La Cloche mountains covered with clouds beyond.

Club island appears to the east, a large fishing station, which we did not visit. The green Rabbit island is also seen. Far off in the Bay, is the long and low Lonely island, a desolate spot to which a tale is attached. It is reported that, somewhere among its rocks, there is a human skeleton in a pine box or rude coffin, but anything more of the poor fellow lying there, under the scream of the gulls and amid the dashing billows, we could not learn. We ran into Tamarack Harbour, a sheltered cove, found a tripod of three sticks, left by former visitors, whereon we hung our kettle and had dinner. This was the only point on the Great Manitoulin touched. Then, across the Bay, for Rattlesnake Harbour, on Fitzwilliam, or Horse island, which stretched before us, large and covered with verdure. Entered this romantic spot at 6 p.m., crossed through the heart-shaped harbour in four fathoms of water and ran upon a stony beach. Behind us was a rising ground covered with small boulders, smooth and polished, and ending in a steep limestone cliff. We had left the Laurentian ranges behind on the north shore. The cliff was full of fissures and little caves. Across the harbour, nets were drying. There was a small shop, a fish-packing and ice house, two or three shanties, then a large tent occupied by a half-breed family, the father a fisherman, with sons who aided him, and two pretty daughters, who have been at school at the Manitowaning Convent, and are now remaining with their father, who is a widower and likes to have his dear ones about him. Beyond that were four conical tepèes, of bark and slabs, occupied by red folk from the Reserve, the squaws making mats of sweet-scented grass and birch bark colored with diamond dyes, girls cleaning fish, and little fellows, fat and jolly, playing themselves. An old Nokomis, blear-eyed, bent and wrinkled, looked out of a tepèe and smiled at us. Pots and drying fish were hung on tripods, over fires before the tents, and, though the weather was warm, a little fire burned on the floor of one of the tents, the smoke circling in it, till it passed out through an opening at the top. Three fishing smacks, belonging to the Indians, lay at the shore; one came in with a fine lot of white fish, taken with a troll, made of a big hook baited with a herring. Nine of these fish weighed 80 pounds when dressed, and were sold at the packing house at three cents a pound. A great raft of logs filled one end of the harbour; a strong tug was working it into shape for a tow to Detroit. We were warned of troublesome neighbours on our side, rattlesnakes from the limestone cliff behind.

A young man was pointed out who had killed thirteen this summer. One of the Bois-brulès girls stepped with a bare foot, on a rattler, but escaped and the deadly rattler was killed by her brother. These reptiles are, in this climate, sluggish and will not attack unless hurt or angered. When roused, they shake their tails and rattle, and then prepare for fight by coiling, and projecting the fangs hidden in their jaws, and as this takes half a minute or so, an agile person can soon jump clear of danger; but woe to him who comes unaware on the angry and alert snake, if the fang strikes a vein or artery!

We had supper on the beach and a quartette played

their favorite game by the camp fire; but we all slept
on board as usual and had snakes in our dreams. The
morning broke with a beautiful sunrise. The playing
quartette were hard to arouse. By 8.30 a.m. we bowled
out amid adieus from our friends on the beach. A
quarter breeze took us along the north side of Horse
island at a great pace, the mainsail had to be lowered,
then the foresail was double reefed, as the mast bent
like a sapling. The Manitoulin shore was soon lost
to view as we wended southward into the open water,
arrived opposite the fine Cove island light at 11.50;
but as there was a stormy sea, passed on and into
the south-west arm of Tobermory harbour. Turning
to the right, we entered, in twelve fathoms, a wonderful
natural harbour. extending half a mile between limestone rocks. Its breadth is one hundred and fifty
yards and depth from three to eight fathoms, unim-
peded with shoal or rock.

No wharves are used, rings are fastened to the natural stone walls and to these vessels are made fast. This
beautiful refuge has, as breakwaters near its mouth,
the small green Doctor island, the large Russell island
and the Flower Pots. This is usually called the 'Big
Tub.' Another bay, the 'Little Tub,' or east arm, is
around a point from the lighthouse. Here are a few
houses, a telegraph office and fish station. We are on
the north end of the Saugeen Peninsula. Under the
clear water of the 'Big Tub' may be seen the ribs of a
large batteau, said to have carried guns eighty years
ago, and to have been sunk and abandoned here when

peace became permanent. The like remains of two old gunboats may be seen in the Penetang harbour. They were sunk after the war of 1812, their guns and tackle being previously removed; a careless way of disposing of them, as they, to some extent, impede navigation, and are hard to raise, when imbedded and waterlogged.

After dinner, four of the party went with guns to Hay harbour to look for game. They lost their way, in returning after nightfall, so retraced their steps back to the water's edge, made a camp fire, slept under an abandoned macinac, and held the fort until morning, when they caught sight of some ducks and two deer. A lynx had enlivened the night with his music. The boys came in tired and hungry, as the breakfast camp fire was blazing.

Struck camp at 9.30, August 13th, and with a good breeze and a couple of tacks, bowled out past the light. The old keeper, a tall man with wrinkled weary face and black pipe, but with his bright girl of ten and barking dog beside him, waved us farewell. Passed between the Doctor and Russell islands, and, to our left, a couple of miles out of course, to observe the Flower Pots, two rocks that rise like great urns at the end of a wooded island. Then struck for Wingfield Basin, where we arrived at 2.30 p m. This is a heart-shaped harbour, lying between high picturesque rocks and woods. It had formerly a fishing station, which was burned. The entrance is not protected and is shoally; its sides are covered with "the panther-peopled forests," and rise in places to hills of some height, wild and unsettled. The growth of trees, shrubs and flowers was very complete. There were vine trellises, garlanded with a species of clematis, and we gathered red pin-cherries, small gooseberries, sugar-plums and pigeon-berries for dessert.

Left at 3 p.m., with fair wind. Cabot's Head and Dyer's Bay are passed, and Cape Croker comes in sight in the blue distance. As we pursue our south-east course, Lion's Head, Barrow Bay, Hope Bay with Barrier island off its mouth, are in the great bay, called Melville Sound, all the east side of the Saugeen Peninsula, so jutting out in long limestone cliffs. Behind is McGregor's harbour. On turning Cape Croker, we ran close-hauled with both sails, south-west, with the three Giants' Steps, large green protuberances on the peninsula, in view. Met the Canada Pacific Railway steamer 'Manitoba,' going north, and entered Colpoy's Bay. Camped on the west side of Hay island.

The critical may ask why two of our number were given names so peculiar, and this may be a suitable time to rise to explain

"Ninety" was a member of the loyal battalion bearing that number during the Riel episode in our North-West. The figure was emblazoned on part of his attire and stood out on his manly breast. He held rank on our trip as "captain of the dingy" "Misery," being the soul of good humor had received that cognomen by way of contradiction. It fitted so well that no other was thought of.

During nearly every day of our sailing, there were hours when our vessel glided smoothly along in the sunshine; while Ernest, the skipper, held the helm, an extempore table was made over the centreboard, on which lunch was spread or "pedro" played. The guitar would then come from its case under the quarter deck, "Ninety's" flute joined in the melody, which floated over the waters, or he would tell us of the gallant dash with his battalion down the woody slope, where the rebel bullets were flying at Batoche. The skipper, too, had his yarns of the bay, and described a sad calamity which he had witnessed but a fortnight ago. A happy party of nine had come from Cape Croker in an Indian Macinac. The vessel had got safely into Wiarton Bay and lay in sight of wharfs and dwellings, when a sudden rushing wind coming down overturned her with the loss of seven of her passengers before help came.

The days of 1812-14 were remembered, when, after the naval engagements on Lake Erie, some of the war schooners came up to these waters, and the boom of their cannon and the shouts of warriors were echoed back by the rocks of the North Channel and the lofty pines and spreading elms along the banks of the Nottawasaga. Then the hardy loyal voyageurs, and their painted and feathered allies, sped in swift canoes over these waters, hundreds of miles through the channels, past the Sault and St. Joseph, to attack the enemy at the Michillimacinac stronghold *(a)*.

(a) See chapter IV.

2

Now each produced his book or pipe, or, when more socially inclined, gave a story or a song.

While all were not equally placid in temperament, or agreed in opinion, it was in good time remembered that "Love is hurt with jar and fret." Little kindnesses and constant consideration were shewn, and he was held a Jonah who disputed. Thus was avoided

> "The little rift within the lute,
> That, by-and-bye, will make the music mute
> And ever widening, slowly silence all." (b)

We were resting in the "White Squall" for the last night, in view of the lights of the Indian houses on Cape Croker.

The moon shone over the water between us and the Cape. The dark green of the trees stood up as a wall behind. An anchor held our vessel's stern so that the waves passed by and broke monotonously on the shore. Jumbo, the little black spaniel, which had been our companion throughout the trip, and well guarded our belongings, lay curled on the deck. For a time the lights of the Indian houses glimmered and then went out. The moon, too, sunk down, Mars, Arcturus and the Pleiades, moved over head ; the tent above the deck protected our couch, and we thought of the lines of the Mohawk poetess Pauline Johnson :

> "O little lake with night-fall interlink't,
> Your darkling shores, your margin indistinct,
> More in your depths' uncertainty there lies
> Than when you image all the sun-set dyes ;
> Like to a poet's soul you seem to be,
> A depth no hand can touch, no eye can see.

(b) Tennyson.

The next morning we prepared our attire for civilized society, then the anchor was hauled in, the sails were set, and with a light wind and many tacks, we made Wiarton in the afternoon.

And now a few words as to the region traversed and its interests.

CHAPTER II.

HISTORICAL AND GEOGRAPHICAL.

AVID THOMPSON was born in West-
minster, England, 30th April, 1770, was
educated as a "Blue-coat School" boy,
and was perhaps a short time at
Oxford. He entered the service
of the Hudson Bay Company, in
October, 1789, and spent the main
part of his life as a surveyor and
astronomer, for that Company
and the North-West Company.
He surveyed the shores of Lake Superior
and passed the Falls of Ste. Marie, in May,
1798. He again visited this region and
surveyed the north shore of that lake in August, 1812.
He then retired, living in Lower Canada for some
time, employed in preparing a map of Western Canada on a scale of fifteen miles to an inch, which map
is in possession of the Ontario Department of Crown
Lands, and is entitled "Map of the North-West Territory of the Province of Canada, 1792-1812, embracing
the region between latitudes 45° and 56° and longi-
(28)

tudes 84° and 124°, made for the North-West Company, 1813-1814."

Mr. Thompson then engaged in defining the boundary, on the part of Great Britain, between Canada and the United States. In 1837 he made a survey of the canal route from Lake Huron to the Ottawa River. He died in Longueil, opposite Montreal, on 10th of February, 1857 at nearly 87 years of age. H. H. Bancroft gives the following account of his personal appearance : "David Thompson was an entirely different order of man from the orthodox fur-trader. Tall and fine-looking, of sandy complexion, with large features, deep-set, studious eyes, high forehead and broad shoulders, the intellectual was well set upon the physical. His deeds have never been trumpeted as those of some others, but in the westward exploration of the North-West Company, no man performed more valuable service, or estimated his achievements more modestly." (a)

Mr. Thompson gives in his journals, now almost a century old, an account of the Georgian Bay, which he treats as the eastern part of Lake Huron. He also left a MS. treatise on the area and drainage of the lakes and rivers of the continent, and as this has not before been in print, we give the part relating to our subject as follows :

" Lake Huron is next in order to Lake Superior, the discharge

(a) A brief narrative of the journeyings of David Thompson in North-Western America, by J. B. Tyrrell, B.A., F.G.S. Proceedings of Canadian Institute, Vol. 24, 135. October, 1888.

of this latter lake is by the Falls of Ste. Marie or more properly rapids, of about three-quarters of a mile in length. Their descent is 15 ft. 10 in., which, with the current below, may give a difference of level of 17 ft., down to Lake Huron. The sides of this lake are, in places, of moderate height, but a great part of them is lowland. By a strait at Cabot's Head, it may be said to be divided into two lakes, the eastern part is called the Georgian Bay. The lake is remarkable for its great number of islands and islets. Of the former, several are large, they lie along the north shore, but the islets are in general small, of low rock, and very many not 100 yards square. Lieutenant Collins, who was on the survey of the lake, counted 47,500 islands and islets. The islets lie so close on the east shore, southward of the French River, that the main shore is not known. The north part of the east side has also much copper ore, its value is not yet known, but accounted the best mine. At the north-west corner of this lake is the once far-famed Island of Michil-a-Mac-a-Naw (The great Tortoise). From its shape it commands the strait to Lake Michigan. The French very early erected a fort and a trading house. The Indians were then very numerous. The country everywhere abounded with game, to and beyond the Mississippi. However dispersed in winter, the then numerous tribes of Indians, early in summer assembled in this island, at times to upwards of two thousand men. A great trade was carried on, French manufactures exchanged for furs, maize, maple-sugar, and some wild rice. The French fort was twice taken and destroyed by strategem. The Indians all declared they had never given permission to erect a fort, which was only a few neat log houses, surrounded by stockades of about 12 feet above the ground, sharp-pointed, with two gates. It was the depository of the goods of the fur traders, from whence they drew the supplies they wanted, as the fur trade required. It was natural to the French garrison to keep their gates closed when such an overwhelming force was on the island, but this the Indians did not pretend to understand, and it is curious to remark, that while the Indians destroyed the fort, the fur traders in their temporary cabins, covered with birch-rind, exposed to every turn of fortune, were respected by the Indians, not the value of a copper was taken from them. The fact is, that had the French garrison thrown open their gates and allowed the Indians free admission to hold their councils and consider the ground to be theirs, however builded upon, all would have been well. But the French brought garrison duty with them, which the Indians could not understand. At the cession of Canada to England, the British took possession of the island, and its trade continued as before, though the Indians were not so numerous, from the small pox, yet the trade was considerable, especially in maple sugar, which was made into what is called muscovado, a close imitation of the West India sugars. The area of Lake Huron is 14,862 square miles."

. . The Georgian Bay has a length from north to south of one hundred and twenty miles. Its southern boundary is 95 miles by rail, north from Toronto, the capital city of the Province of Ontario. The 46th parallel of north latitude passes along its upper end; on either side are the 86th and 82nd meridians of west longitude, its average breadth being 50 miles. It is separated from Lake Huron by the Saugeen Peninsula and the Grand Manitoulin Island. Between these is a channel through which the Canadian Pacific Company's steamers and other vessels pass on their course to the upper lake ports. There is another passage, the North Channel, between the Grand Manitoulin and the north shore, and on this, at the north-west corner of the bay, is the Village of Killarney.

The bay has, on its south shore, the important towns

of Collingwood, Thornbury, Meaford, Owen Sound
and Wiarton ; on the east, are Penetanguishene and
Midland. Near the last is the site of the old Fort
Ste. Marie on the Wye, occupied by the Jesuit Fathers
and their Huron converts, 243 years ago. Twenty miles
from them, are the Christian Islands, to which they
were driven by the ferocious Iroquois, who still pur-
sued and harried them to destruction. Here too are
the remains of another Fort Ste. Marie, put up by the
fugitives on the island. History has no sadder tale
than that of the weary exodus, from the rude wilderness home they loved so well, across these waters under
the command of Father Ragueneau, on the 14th of
June, 1649. The flames flew up over the fort and
refuge they left, consuming in half an hour, the
work of nine or ten years. They passed down the
Wye into the bay, only to meet more trials, disaster
and death. (*a*)

From the "Shining sands" of Penetanguishene, as
the name implies, Sir John Franklin passed on St.
George's Day, 23rd April, 1823, to join his party on
his second journey to the shores of the Polar Sea.
His party comprised thirty-three men in two large
canoes provided by the Hudson Bay Company, and
they paddled over the bay we have described, and
along the Grand Manitoulin, to Sault Ste. Marie,
where they arrived on the first of May.

Penetanguishene is now a town of some importance,
easily reached by rail from Toronto. A Roman Cath-

(*a*) Relation des Jesuites, par le Pere Paul Ragueneau, 1650.

olic church commemorates the Jesuit martyrs. A large hotel, having a beautiful outlook over the bay and spacious grounds, attracts many summer visitors. Near this is the well-conducted juvenile prison or reformatory for boys.

Penetanguishene was, during the troubles with the United States, of 1812-14, a Royal Naval Station. Barracks for soldiers and marines, and store-houses for supplies, were erected here, and for some years after, these quarters were occupied by a few army veterans. Armed vessels took their departure from this port for the protection of British interests on lakes Huron and Superior.

It cannot be doubted that the Georgian Bay is of strategic interest from a military point of view. It is on the water route through the upper lakes and has now the Canada Pacific Railway at no great distance from its easterly and northerly shores. The Manitoulin group shields it and the North Channel from exposure. Its islands and inlets afford cover and concealment for vessels and there are no better sailors than the hardy fishermen upon these waters.

It was with much interest that, as we moved away from the Minks, a hale old sailor was pointed out. He was standing before a new shanty, his white hair blown by the breeze, and we were told that he was in one of the later polar exploration expeditions and could spin many an interesting yarn about ice-floes, white bears and walrus, but our sails were full and we could only salute him at a distance. Passing

north, we came to the beautiful village of Parry
Sound and along this shore are, on islands and penin-
sulas, the vacation cottages of families from Toronto
and elsewhere, who, with sail or steam craft, or in
house-boats, enjoy in summer the most exhilarating
of fresh air, and pleasures only to be found around
the camp fire, and at an elevation of 578 feet above
the sea.   The Ottawa, Arnprior and Parry Sound
Railway, now in process of construction, will make
Parry Sound an important port on a direct route
between Chicago and Montreal.   It is opposite the
main channel through which vessels come from lakes
Huron and Superior, and it is almost due west from
Ottawa.   At the north-east end of the bay is French
River, which was so impeded with logs as to hinder
our passage through it to the rapids and falls a few
miles above. which impede further navigation. Other
visitors may be more fortunate.   It unites the waters
of the bay with Lake Nippissing. A Government surveyor says of it : "The scenery of the Thousand Isles
of the St. Lawrence is tame and uninteresting as compared with the endless variety of island and bay,
granite cliff, and deep sombre defile, which mark the
character of the beautiful solitary French River."

The Grand Manitoulin is a beautiful island, in length
80 miles and in breadth 20 miles, with numerous inlets.
It has various elevations on its surface, but none more
than 350 feet above the level of Lake Huron.

The names of places, met about the Georgian Bay,
remind us of the ancient inhabitants, and indicate the

land whence its present people came. Some, such as Ossosané, an important Huron village on the east side of the bay in early days, are forgotten. Later Indian names are mostly of Ottawa, Chippewa or Iroquois origin. A township in the County of Peel bears the name of the Chippewa chief, Chinguacosè, which means "The Small Pine." The Jesuits left many spots called after saints, such as Ste. Marie on the Wye and Ste. Marie on St. Joseph, the chief Christian island. These islands were also in later days called Faith, Hope and Charity. They are occupied by an excellent body of Christian Chippewas.

In the centre of the Huron territory, between Waubashene Bay and Lake Simcoe, were St. Louis and St. Ignace, where Brebeauf and Lalemant, Jesuit missionaries, suffered martyrdom at the stake. When this beautiful region was mapped out, nearly two centuries later, into three townships, a governor's lady was requested to name them, "Pray call them after my dear little pet dogs," she said ; so they were christened Flos, Tiny and Tay. The great bay bears the name of royalty. French River was so named because of the nationality of the early white traders. This river would with propriety be called by its ancient name, The Nipissing. Lake Simcoe and its surrounding county also are so called from the first Governor of Upper Canada, the loyal General John Graves Simcoe, Commander of the famous corps, the "Queen's Rangers," in the American Revolutionary War. The adjoining county from Earl Grey, Barrie, the chief town of the County

Simcoe, bears the name of a brave naval hero, as
does its bay, that of the ill-fated Captain Kempen-
feldt, who went down at his post on the *Royal George*
off Spithead, 29th August, 1782, as sung in the verses
of Cowper.

> " His sword was in its sheath,
> His fingers held the pen,
> When Kempenfeldt went down,
> With twice four hundred men."

The road leading from Toronto to Lake Simcoe was
mainly opened out by the Rangers, many of whom
settled along it, and is called Yonge Street from the
Engineer officer in charge of its construction. The
naming of a mountain, river, lake or town was too
often esteemed a light matter, and the significant
Indian names were forgotten or discarded in favor of
a local magnate, or for some merely casual circumstances. Yet we have an historical nomenclature of
good proportions. The Crimea gave Alma and Ink-
erman ; Port Arthur and Fort William are called from
the present dynasty. Confining our remarks to the
Bay, we find Cockburn island in the Manitoulin group,
called after the naval officer by whose command the
city of Washington was burned in 1814, in retaliation
for the destruction of our little town of Niagara and
other places on our frontier. Drummond island reminds us of the hero of Lundy's Lane, a battle fought
from sunset to midnight within a short distance
of the Niagara Cataract. Captain Parry, R.N., has
given his name to the Sound, island, and district

through which the rivers Muskoka, Musquosh and Meganetawan pass to the Georgian Bay. The inlet at the mouth of the last named river is named from the unfortunate Admiral Byng; the town of Collingwood from Nelson's second in command at Trafalgar, Owen Sound from Captain Owen, R.N. The English peers St. Edmund, Sydenham, Albemarle and Derby gave their names to townships on the south and west of the Bay; and on Manitoulin island, Lords Cockburn, Campbell and Carnarvon are similarly remembered. Franklin island commemorates the daring north sea navigator, who, as stated, passed through this Bay on the way to undertake his second Arctic voyage. Cabot's Head reminds us of the famous Venetian family, of whom Giovanni was the head, and of his son Sebastian, who was distinguished both in the Spanish service and in that of Britain under Henry VIII. and Edward VI. It is indeed claimed that he discovered the American continent some months before it was seen by Columbus. Sir John Barrow, the author, and for many years Secretary of the Admiralty, gave his name to Barrow Bay, in front of which is the cape called after the Scottish family of Dundas.

The Manitoulin Island Railway, soon to be built from Nelson on the Canada Pacific Railway, across the La Cloche islands to the village of Little Current, and thence to Gore Bay and other places on the Grand Manitoulin, will make that important island easily accessible at all seasons.

The "Temporary Judicial District of Manitoulin"

comprises the Great Manitoulin island, the islands named Cockburn, Barrie, Fitzwilliam, Lonely, Club, Wall, and Rabbit, and the small islands lying between any of these and the Great Manitoulin. Sittings of General Sessions of the Peace and of Division Courts are held in the Grand Manitoulin. The telegraph was, late in 1892, extended across from the mainland, and this group of islands will, ere many years pass, occupy the full status of a judicial county or district. *(a)*

(a) See the Ontario Statute of 1888, 51 Vic. ch. 14: The Indian status and government will continue to coëxist as explained in Chap. IV.

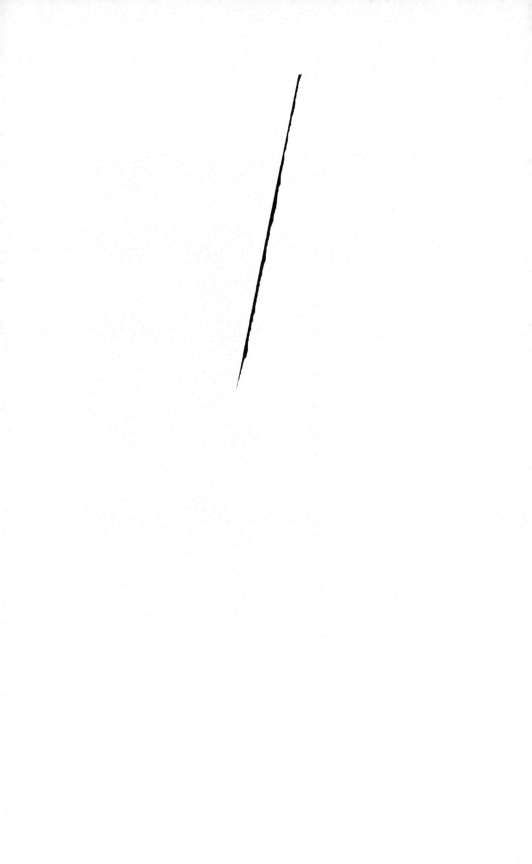

In the Surgeon Bay Aug 1848

CHAPTER III.

GEOLOGICAL FORMATION AND MINING INTERESTS.

FROM the village of Killarney, at the north-west corner of the Georgian Bay, to the river Severn at its south-eastern end, is a stretch of land covered with original forest trees, supported by a soil formed of layers of leaf-mould underlaid by Archæan rocks, granites, gneisses, and overflows often known as the Upper Laurentian formation. Rivers descend to the Bay here and there, forming points, small bays and coves. The shore is fringed with innumerable islands, often so numerous that the actual coast line is hidden from view. The islands of the Bay, large and small, are estimated to be fully thirty thousand, some of them of considerable size

(39)

and wooded, but most of them of small dimensions
and having only a thin vegetation. Along the north
shore, the mass of islands extends for some ten miles
into the Bay. The channels between them are the
chosen breeding grounds for the white fish, here
caught in immense quantities, as also for the large
lake trout, sturgeon and other fish. The islands are
of granite, syenite, gneiss, or trap, with an occasional
limestone peculiar to this formation. The Laurentian
sub-structure extends south-easterly to the Severn
and generally north and north-east, far beyond the
boundaries of the Province. Bedded in this, are found
near the mouth of the Ottawa the great graphite,
apatite and mica deposits, producing rich out-puts of
mineral, disclosing untold wealth for the future.

The Laurentian formations form, as far as we know,
the foundations of the earth's crust and are separable
from the rocks lying above them. The Lower Laurentian is held to be the oldest and deepest the world
over. The Upper formation has been estimated to
be fully twenty miles in thickness in the Ottawa
valley. It discloses sixty-one species of mineral, the
Lower barely any.

Most geologists admit that no fossils have been
found in the Laurentians, which some interpret as
indicating their igneous origin. The " folding process "
of the earth's crust can be seen to advantage in the
Huronian formation, commencing at its south-east
boundary a little west of Killarney. In that it is
usual to find a layer of one kind of rock overlapping

another of a different kind. Great volcanic activity took place during the Huronian period. Ashes, tufa broken rock and other matters were thrown out, often with explosive, violence. Evidence of water abiding on the earth's surface now appears, and of the wear and tear of the sea on the solid rocks. The surface remained covered by shallow seas, hot and full of dissolved mineral matter and unfit to support animal or vegetable life.

" As a rule the Huronian rocks are less contorted, or corrugated on the small scale, than the Laurentian, but on a large scale they partake of the same foldings which have affected the latter."

" The Huronian occurs in the midst of the Laurentian in the form of more or less completely separated areas, or with straggling connections between them."

" Huronian rocks often occupy spaces with elongated or even angular out-lines in the midst of the Laurentian areas, both sets of rocks having been thrown by pressure into sharp folds, standing at high angles to the horizon, the Huronian often appear to dip under the older Laurentian, but this is merely the effect of over-turning and does not shew that a part of the Laurentian is newer than the locally underlying Huronian." *(a)*

The most extensive Huronian formation in Ontario

(a) Professor Bell in report of Royal Mineral Commission of Ontario, 1890, p. 7 and 17 ; also in the report of the Provincial Bureau of Mines, 1891 ; p. 63.

3

is that north of the Georgian Bay, extending from Killarney north-east crossing the Canadian Pacific Railway in the immense Algoma district.

The great copper and nickel deposits are in this region. The Director of the Dominion Geological survey, Dr. A. R. C. Selwyn, in his evidence before the Ontario Mineral Commission in 1890, states that the " Western limit of the Huronian area is on the upper branches of the Vermilion and Spanish Rivers. Everywhere I know of in Eastern Ontario, gold is associated with the Huronian rocks. Wherever they occur, you are likely to find gold-bearing veins and other mineral deposits."

Were we to go, on the north shore, a few hundred miles west of the Georgian Bay, we would come to the Bruce and Wellington Mines, worked for thirty years ending in 1876, during which copper ore taken out was estimated to be worth more than $6,000,000. The work was only discontinued owing to the low price of that metal. High smoke stacks and large buildings, surrounded by a mountain of mineral debris, are seen now on the place formerly so busy and full of the noise of blast furnaces and rendering mills. The price of copper remains so low that it is being more extensively used in building and other mechanical work. The eave-troughs and rain conductors of the new parliament, and other public buildings in Toronto are made of it.

The Ophir Gold Mine is in the township of Galbraith, fifteen miles north of the Bruce Mines, between the Missisauga and Thesalon rivers. It is owned by Duluth capitalists. The ore is in a bluish quartz. There are two veins. A depth of 100 feet has been reached. The indications are promising.

Persons connected with this work, have tested the tailings of the Bruce Mines and found considerable traces of gold in them, so that it is not improbable that they may be worked over for the richer metal. Dr. Selwyn states, "They are now finding gold-bearing veins down the Thesalon and all through that region, from the north shore of the Georgian Bay to north of Sudbury."

The Silver Islet mine, on Thunder Cape in Lake Superior, was worked from 1870 to 1884, reaching a depth of 1230 feet. The value of the out-put of silver was $3,250,000. The vein still continues unexhausted but the shaft is filled with water which flooded the mine. (*a*)

One of the most interesting and remarkable features of the country north of the Georgian Bay is a basin of Cambrian formation, extending from the west side of Lake Wahnapitae to the centre of Trill township, a distance of thirty-six miles, with a breadth of

---

(*a*) An excellent account of the Silver Islet Mine, an undertaking of historic interest, is given in the evidence of the late Mr. A. J. Cattanach, in the report of the Royal Commission of 1890, p. 195. Mr. Simon J. Dawson, C.E., M.P., also there gives his opinion as to it and other important North-Shore mines, concluding thus : "Where work has been done systematically, it has been very satisfactory, and where mines have been abandoned and work stopped, it has generally been on account of the want of capital." As to the Bruce and Wellington copper mines, see the evidence of Wm. and W. H. Plummer, in same report, p. 101.

eight miles in its broadest part. This formation can
be best observed in the southern part of the township
of Balfour, and has attracted the attention of eminent
geologists. Proceeding from the crossing of the Vermilion River by the main line of the Canada Pacific
Railway, a walk southward of two miles on the Government Road, brings the traveller to a noticeable
ridge of black slate and conglomerate. This ridge is
a quarter of a mile in width ; on one of its sides is
seen a volcanic breccia, on the other an agglome-
rate schist. Dr. Bell refers to this in the Ontario
Report of 1891. Prof. Geo. H. Williams has examined
the breccia and says it is composed of sharply angular
fragments of volcanic glass and pumice, which still
preserve every detail of their original form. " The
fragments, even down to those of the smallest dimensions, have the angular form characteristic of glass
shreds produced by explosive eruptions."

" After a careful study of this rock, I find it possible only to interpret it as a remarkable instance of a
very ancient volcanic glass-breccia, preserved through
the lucky accident of silicification. Nor did this process go on, as is usual through devitrification and loss
of structure, but rather like the gradual replacement
of many silicified woods whose every minute detail of
structure is preserved. The rarity of such rocks in the
earth's oldest formations is readily intelligible ; but,
for this very reason, the exceptional preservation of
a rock like this is all the more welcome proof that
explosive volcanic activity took place at the surface,

then as now, and on a scale, if possible, greater than that with which we are familiar." (*a*)

NICKEL.—This most important of Ontario ores, was known to the Chinese. Baktrian coins, bearing the inscription of King Euthodymus, who lived 200 B.C., are found almost identical in composition with the nickel coins of the present day. It is often found in meteorites in conjunction with iron, cobalt, silver, copper, phosphorus and other materials; the iron is generally the chief component, but in the meteorite from Octebbeha, the nickel was 60 per cent. and iron 30 per cent. of the mass. German miners endeavored in vain to produce copper out of nickeliferous mineral, and angrily called the product, *kupfer-nickel*, or copper-devil, which name it still bears.

In 1751 Cronstedt showed the true nature of this metal, but his views were controverted until, in 1775, celestial aid was given to settle the argument. Many meteors containing considerable quantities of nickel fell in various places, and these being analyzed, its existence as a distinct metal was admitted, and its properties became better understood.

Nickel is found in combination with oxygen as Bunsenite, with carbon as Texasite, but its most important position is as a silicate, and in conjunction with other metals, in various shapes and under many names. The physical properties of nickel make it of great value; one gram can be drawn out into 600

(*a*) Bulletin of Geological Society of America, 1890, p. 138.

feet of wire. It can be welded on iron or steel with a covering of only .00039 inch. Its strength is greater than that of iron and equal to that of Bessemer steel. It does not oxydize at ordinary temperatures, even in moist air. Reference will be made to the important qualities nickel possesses and imparts as an alloy with steel, and which are only now becoming fully understood. (*a*)

Nickel enters into the composition of coins of most countries of the world. In Germany cooking utensils have lately been made of pure nickel. In the arts it is used, alloyed with copper and zinc in making *German silver;* the same metals with a percentage of iron, make *silverine,* and with silver *argent de Mousset* is made.

The most productive nickel mines heretofore, have been those of New Caledonia. Their ore contained from seven to fifteen per cent. of metal. The means of removing the matte to the sea coast, having been improved ; ores of less value are there mined now with profit.

The Ontario nickel mines, though in their infancy, are as perfect in their equipment, and as scientifically managed as any in the world. As the uses for nickel increase, this industry will still further develop. It is already one of great importance and promises to reach vast proportions.

(*a*) The discovery of the process was announced simultaneously by J. F. Hale, of Sheffield, and M. Marbeau, of France, in the journal of the Iron and Steele Institute, No. 1, 1881.

There are three great nickel belts in the Sudbury district; the first extending from the township of Carson, through the townships of Blezard, McKim and Snider. In this are the Blezard, Sheppard, Murray, Copper-Cliff, Evans and Stobie mines. The last three are the property of the Canadian Copper Company. The Dominion Mineral Company works on lot 4 range 2 of Blezard, a mile north of the Stobie mine. Near these, and in the same run, are the Russell and McConnell locations. The second belt runs for several miles almost parallel to the Sault branch of the Canada Pacific Railway. The third extends from Geneva Lake through the townships of Moncrief and Craig, and the unsurveyed territory to the north. It is crossed by the railway about forty-eight miles west of the Spanish River near Blue Water Lake. All these belts run north-east and south-west. In addition, there are several important minor belts, such as that near Lake Wahnapitae and those in the townships of Graham, Denison, Drury, Hyman and Nairn. It is estimated that more than four-fifths of the known nickel deposits of the world are in this region, so that the Georgian Bay district has a practical monopoly of the world's supply of this useful metal.

The ore is much the same wherever occurring in the Sudbury district, being a mixture of nickeliferous pyrhotite, or magnetic pyrites, with the chalcopyrite or copper pyrites. The usual site of the formations is at the junction of greenstone with some other rock, such as granite, gneiss or felsite.

The word 'greenstone' is used by geologists to include a variety of trappean rocks which can not always be distinguished from one another in the field. In the Sudbury district they consist of diabases diorites and gabbros. (*a*)

All the deposits of nickeliferous copper ore of the district, examined, says Dr. Bell, occur in diorite rocks, and in most cases the diorite is brecciated or holds angular and also rounded fragments of all sizes of rocks of various kinds, the prevailing varieties being other kinds of diorite, quartz-syenites, crystalline schists, grey-wacké and quartzites. The general geological position of these ores is therefore in diorite and more especially brecciated diorite with either gneiss or quartz-syenite near one side. (*b*)

The occurrence of dykes of crystalline diabase near some of the deposits is noted as remarkable. These dykes cut through all the stratified Huronian rocks of the district. Some run west, north-west, others south-west, and one at the outlet of Ramsay lake, runs about west, or towards the Copper-Cliff mine. The composition of the dykes is newer than any of the rocks through which they pass, and appears on microscopical examination, to be apparently identical with the diabase overflow of the Animikie formation of Lake Superior, which includes the silver producing rocks. The various nickeliferous ores have been analyzed by Mr. C. T. Mixer and described by Mr. S. H.

(*a*) Dr. Bell, Report of Bureau of Mines, 1891, p. 75.
(*b*) Dr. Bell, Royal Commission, Ont., 1890, p. 434.

Emmens, the able expert of the Emmens Metal Company, who has given a table exhibiting the composition of each. FOLGERITE is so named after Commodore Folger, chief of the United States Bureau of Ordnance, in recognition of his distinguished services in the utilization of nickel-steel.

In BLUEITE we find the name of Mr. A. Blue, director of Ontario mines. WHARTONITE is named after Mr. Joseph Wharton, of Camden, N. J., on account of his position as head of the nickel industry in America. The table indicates the relations of the known nickel and nickel iron sulphides to each other. Of the very high grade species given, specimens are but rare, the four of lesser grade are the staples of the mines of Sudbury.

MESSRS. EMMENS AND MIXER'S TABLE.

Nickel and Nickel Iron Sulphides. (a)

NAME.	PERCENTAGE CONSTITUTION.			MOLECULAR CONSTITUTION.			
	Ni.	Fe	S	Ni S	Ni S$_2$	Fe S	FeS$_2$
Millerite	64.72	......	35.28	1	..	..	
Polydymite...	59.47	......	40.53	3	1	..	
Beyrichite....	57.90	......	42.10	2	1	..	
Ferriferous.... Polydymite...	44.92	14.26	40.82	3	..	..	1
Folgerite	32.87	31.30	35.83	1	..	1	
Pentlandite...	22.03	41.95	36.02	1	..	2	
Horbachite ...	11.24	42.81	45.95	1	1	1	1
Inverarite	10.44	49.72	39.84	1	..	4	1
Whartonite...	6.10	40.68	53.22	..	1	..	7
Blueite..	3.76	42.96	53.28	..	1	..	12

(a) See Canadian Mining Review of Ottawa, volume 12, page 6, January, 1893, for Mr. Emmens' article and this table.

In this table no mention is made of a valuable and new mineral in Canada, Gersdorffite, found in the third concession of Denison township. Assays of this have given fifty-five per cent. of nickel. Analyses of twenty European samples made by Dana average 29.77 per cent. of nickel.

In the able paper by Mr. George Mickle of Toronto read before the Canadian Institute (a) it is shown that the Sudbury nickeliferous deposits increase in richness as depth is reached, and it is noteworthy that this conclusion has so far been verified in every case by practical experience. Mr. Mickle closes his paper with the assertion that the Ontario nickel mines will in time assume the position which those of New Caledonia have occupied heretofore.

Mr. J. M. Clark, LL.B., of Toronto, is of the same opinion. He is well versed in the mineralogy of this region. Mr. Archibald Blue, the accomplished director of the Ontario Bureau of Mines, states in his official report for 1891, referred to, that nickel is the most important of all our ores, and that there are inexhaustible supplies of it in the country north of the Georgian Bay. Fifty years ago nickel was found with copper on what is known as the Wallace location near the mouth of Whitefish river. The properties of the metal were then little known or appreciated. The proprietors of the location left it in charge of an honest man who agreed to watch over it until

(a) Notes on Nickel by Geo. Mickle, B.A., 20th March, 1891. Transactions of Canadian Institute, vol. 11, p. 77.

they returned to develop the property. Year after year passed but they did not return. For a time his wages were sent him, but for many years he received no pay, yet held his shanty at the river's mouth and made his living by hunting or fishing. When met by the voyageur or Indian, passing down the White-fish river, or paddling along the north shore, with his gun and traps or net, it was known that he was re-turning to his charge, and so, for nearly forty years, his lonely watch was kept until new proprietors came. Little did the simple-minded sentinel dream of the wonderful spirit hidden under the dark rocks, the "Copper-devil," destined at last to emerge there and at Sudbury, clad in armour of Vulcan, able to resist the force of cannon of the heaviest calibre.

The construction of the Canadian Pacific Railway led to the important discoveries that have been made in the district of which Sudbury is the centre. When blasting an open cut four miles north-west of Sudbury, the engineers struck an unusually hard and trouble-some rock. On investigation it proved to be nickel-iferous. H. H. Vivian & Co., of Swansea, Wales, secured this property, now known as the "Murray Mine," and many shipments of matte have been made to Wales. By the use of approved methods a matte containing 35 per cent. of nickel has been secured. A large working force is employed. The Canadian Cop-per Company have erected Bessemer furnaces and are so enabled to greatly increase the per-centage. The Director of Mines states generally as to this nickel region, that " Eight mines are being worked, three large smelting plants are in operation."

Commodore Folger and Lieutenant Buckingham, two officers of the United States navy department, made an early visit to the Sudbury district and after inspecting, reported many millions of tons of ore in sight. The value of nickel when united with steel, producing an alloy which combines hardness, strength and freedom from fracture under heavy blows, has been so amply demonstrated, that both the British Admiralty and United States navy have decided to use it largely. Their example has been quickly followed by other European countries, notably France and Germany.

During the year 1890 the United States Secretary of the Navy obtained 4,536 tons of nickel matte from Sudbury, containing one-fifth that number of tons of nickel, which were used in the conducting of a series of experiments, by which the value of the alloy as armour for ships has been amply demonstrated. The reports of the United States Secretary of the Navy for 1891 and 1892 give detailed statements of the experiments made. Early in 1889 the department had decided to use all-steel plating. Subsequently its attention had been directed to the possibilities of nickel-steel as a material for armour. Professor Jas. Riley had raised the question in a paper read before the Iron and Steel Institute in May, 1889. The promise held out, says Mr. Secretary Tracy, seemed too great to be ignored by a government requiring 20,000

tons of armour for its new fleet. Then followed at
Annapolis in September 1890, the trial of compound
and all-steel plates of amazing strength, but they
were shattered to pieces by projectiles from the
eight-inch gun used, while the nickel-steel, though
slightly more penetrable than the all-steel, remained
unbroken, and "the integrity of the plate as the covering of a ship's side was practically as perfect at the
close of the trial as if no shot had been fired." (Report
of 1892, p. 16).

Other tests took place in October and November,
1891, and in July, 1892. At the last a plate of "Harveyized" nickel-steel, $10\frac{1}{2}$ inches thick, was fired at
with five Holtzer forged steel shells out of an eight-
inch gun. All these shells were smashed on the surface of the plate, which showed little sign of injury.

In consequence of the high efficiency of nickel-steel,
so demonstrated, Congress appropriated $1,000,000
for the purchase of nickel matte, which the territory
of the United States, as far as known, did not afford.
Contracts were then made with the Canadian Copper
Company, for the delivery at Sudbury of this material, which should contain not less than an average
of fifteen per cent. of nickel.

The U. S. Navy report shows that the Canadian
Company received for nickel ore sold to the United
States Government in 1891, $321,322. They are
stated to have received more than $400,000 in 1892.
The Secretary of the Navy claims in his report for
1891, that the "nickel Harveyized plate" and the

high carbon nickel plate, used in the test, proved superior to all the foreign plates used at the Annapolis trial, and that "the high carbon Harveyized plate is undoubtedly the best armour plate ever subjected to ballistic test." A triumphant spirit pervades the Secretary's reports as he sings pæans in praise of American steel when tempered by Canadian nickel. The proportion of nickel used in making this armour is $3\frac{1}{4}$ per cent.

The work is done for the Government at the great establishments of Carnegie, Phipps & Co , and of the Bethlehem Iron Company.

The Carnegie Company are now constructing several immense furnaces at their works in Homestead, Pennsylvania, for use solely in the making of nickel-steel armour plate.

The Cleveland, Ohio, Rolling Mill Company caused important experiments to be made during the autumn of 1892, under direction of an experienced French engineer, to determine the relative quality of steel, with and without the addition of nickel. The deductions from the results obtained are stated to be as follows: (1) Nickel-steel has an average higher limit of elasticity of more than thirty per cent. (2) Its tensile strength is increased over unalloyed steel by about twenty per cent., and (3) the ductility is not reduced by the presence of nickel.

The public and domestic uses to which this alloy will be put are constantly increasing. The Director of the Bureau looks forward to great activity in the working of the Ontario nickel mines, and with this anticipates an awakening interest in the mining and smelting of iron also, of which there are ample stores in this region.

GOLD MINING.—Reference has been made to gold mining on the Thesalon river, some thirty miles north of the Georgian Bay. A series of quartz veins has been found, which may in time play an important part in the mineral history of Canada. Most of these veins are within a triangle formed by the main line of the Canadian Pacific Railway, its branch to Sault Ste. Marie and the western boundary of Fairbank township produced. In the centre of this triangle is a remarkable lake, more than one hundred feet higher than the Vermilion river into which it is emptied by a stream less than a mile in length. This is called Gordon Lake from J. R. Gordon, C. E., the engineer who explored the district.

The largest of these veins, proved to be more or less auriferous, presents, as Mr. J. M. Clark states, a remarkable spectacle. The lead of quartz can be traced for several miles, ranging in width from 15 to 150 feet. Its strike is north 10° east, and the dip about 40°. On an outcrop of the vein, a mile east of the Vermilion, a shaft has been sunk to a depth of 112 feet, and from this, drifts have been run, all in vein matter, white quartz, popularly known as "California quartz." Though the produce is of low grade, it is stated to be of large quantity. There are three other like veins in the townships of Fairbank and Creighton. Similar indications are found in adjoining townships. The work of development has given very encouraging results, and those interested regard the future of these deposits with sanguine anticipations.. One of these gold veins is found about half a mile south of Vermilion lake in the township of Fairbank. The others are in the vicinity of Gordon lake. The ore is said to be free-milling and easily treated. A mining expert of extensive American experience, who has examined these localities, affirms that several of the quartz veins in Fairbank strongly resemble the Homestake mines of the Black Hills. Modern improvements, in methods and means for reducing and treating ores, have so diminished the cost, that gold ore of the character found in the district north of the Georgian Bay can be mined, milled and treated for less than $3 a ton. The mining of these veins gives employment to about one hundred men at present.

PLATINUM.—Next in interest to the gold deposits, are the platiniferous ore of this region. It is found either in a free state, or in a curious chemical compound first discovered here and called Sperrylite. Professor H. L. Wells, of Yale College, examined a specimen of such ore, from the Vermilion mine in Denison township, in 1889, and declared it to be a distinct mineral species, containing 52.57 per cent. of platinum. It has since been found, in limited quantity, in the Huronian formation. A platiniferous vein runs for several miles east and west, about two miles south of the main line of the Canada Pacific Railway, through the townships of Balfour, Dowling and Fairbank. Rich traces of this metal, now more valuable than gold, are also stated to be found west of Sudbury, along the Sault branch of the railway. Traces of antimony, rhodium, and palladium are found with the platinum. Other metals, including tin, lead, copper, and zinc, have been discovered in this region. No doubt some of them will be found in considerable and profitable quantity.

The Huronian area, like the Laurentian, is destitute of all trace of organic life, unless it be the "Eozoon Canadense," claimed by Sir W. Dawson to have been of that character. The name owes its origin to Sir Charles Lyell, and refers to the dawn of being. Many geological authorities, including Professor Bell, treat this as a scientific myth. The Huronian is Archaean or Azoic, and its origin is attributed largely to volcanic action. The term Huronian, derived from Lake Huron, was given by the Geological Survey officers, forty years ago, and has been understood to include all the rocks lying between the Laurentian below it and the Cambrian or earliest fossiliferous rocks above. The prevailing dark green and grey colors offer a marked contrast to the lighter greys and reddish greys of the Laurentian.

Leaving the south boundary of the Upper Laurentian, a few miles south of the little Severn River, which is the outlet of Lake Simcoe into the Georgian Bay, the "Bird's eye" formation presents itself. The term is derived from a fossil found in these rocks.

4

It consists of bluish and dark grey limestones, with interstratified grey shales. It occurs on some of the islands on the North Channel also, and skirts the southern edge of the Laurentian area, from Penetanguishene to Kingston. The width of this deposit is but a few miles. Building and lithographic stone is derived from it.

Next easterly is a belt of Trenton limestone, Lake Simcoe is imbedded in it. The Christian Islands are formed of it and it crops out at Little Current on the Grand Manitoulin. It affords excellent building stone and is valuable for natural gas and petroleum. This formation extends eastward to Kingston on Lake Ontario and appears again at Ottawa, the cliffs about the Capital being formed of it. Adjoining the Trenton on the west is a narrow belt of Utica shale, the name being derived from a town in New York State. Tarry oil was distilled from this shale, which yielded three to four per cent. of its weight at a cost of fourteen cents per gallon. When free petroleum was discovered in Canada in 1858, this enterprise was abandoned. Still passing westward from Collingwood is the Hudson River formation, about 700 feet thick, which consists of drab marls, clays and shales, interbedded with layers of limestone and sandstone.

Next is a belt of Medina red and green marls, with a fine grained light grey, sometimes reddish sandstone, called the "grey band," at top. This and the Clinton formation, both being named from places in New York State, extend to Owen Sound.

Lastly, as we surround the Bay, comes a great belt of Niagara limestone, having a thickness of 400 feet. It is one of the most marked fossil deposits in the Province. It forms the sides of the gorge of Niagara Falls, whose waters have cut through the limestone 164 feet, and half as far below it into the black shale beneath. This formation then curves, past and under the west end of Lake Ontario, through five counties, and in its northerly course becomes the Blue Mountains in the county of Grey, rising 1200 feet over Lake Huron, or 1800 feet above the sea, and is the main formation of the Saugeen Peninsula and Manitoulin Islands. It is valuable building stone and burns to good lime. The geological terms used are those found in the report of the Ontario Royal Commission of 1890, though American geologists now generally class under Archaean both the Laurentian and Huronian. Laurentian includes the Archaic gneisses and granites; Huronian includes secondary granites, quartzites and slates. Beside these come old sandstones, with conglomerates of various kinds.

On these Archaean rocks, which were at some period more submerged than they are now, the Silurian sea deposited limestone, so that the Lower Silurian, or Ordovician, and Huronian often lie on each other, with a bed of iron or quartz between. The west side of the Bay is, as has been shown, Silurian, the north and east Azoic; but here and there an outlier of limestone crops out on the Azoic side, as evidence that it once extended across the Bay.

It is thought, by Spencer and others, that there was a pre-glacial river entering the Bay north of the Indian Peninsula, and passing down by Collingwood through Lake Simcoe into Lake Ontario, near Port Hope.

Great numbers of lakes are found in all Canadian areas of Laurentian and Huronian formation. From one-half to one-third of the surface is covered with water. Through vast regions, these lakes, from 100 miles in length, to the size of ponds, exist in thousands.

They are generally in chains or groups, and form the means of travelling by canoe, with connections by streams and occasional portages, in any direction. Each watercourse is connected with those on either side, by trails made and worn in the soil by wild animals—deer, moose, caribou, bear and foxes. The Indians used them as they sought game, stealing along silently on soft moccasins or snow shoes, or journeyed with canoe raised over the head. The trail remains visible, especially when protected by overhanging trees, for years after wild animals have ceased to use it as their run-way. These narrow winding courses are trod with security by the explorer, hunter and voyageur, as they know they are sure to lead to some part of the watercourses. In maps of the new townships, the trails are indicated by dotted lines. In the prairies of the West they are followed by the half-breeds' creaking ox-cart.

Falls, some of them of considerable height, cascades

and rapids, are found in the rivers and streams, connecting the lakes, of great variety and beauty. While there is no tide in these inland waters, yet when the wind prevails with strength for a few hours, it causes a rush of water from one inlet to another. There is an instance of this at the Minks Islands, where a long narrow channel between high basaltic sides, ran during our visit like a mill-race, and a village on the Grand Manitoulin is called Little Current, from a like phenomenon on a larger scale.

From various causes a breeze is seldom wanting on the bay. The yachtsman will never lie long becalmed on its surface.

Numerous places throughout the area we have circumscribed, have marks of extensive glaciation, which took place in these Archæan regions during the drift period. The surface of the rocks bears these ice marks in flutings, furrows and grooves, and these are as plain on the tops of the hills as in the valleys. Not only have the beds of streams and ponds been so hollowed out, but the basins of the lakes have been enlarged by glacial action.

In the metamorphic regions in the northern parts of Ontario, says Dr. Bell (a) the rounded glaciated surfaces of the tops and sides of the hills have been left almost or quite bare in some parts. In most places the smoothed and grooved or striated rock surfaces are covered by a thick deposit of stiff clay, mixed with sand, gravel, stones and boulders. This is known

(a) Ont. Mineral Report 1890. 49.

as boulder-clay or hard pan. In Scotland it is called *till*, and this name is being generally adopted. An erroneous impression attributed these phenomena to icebergs, but says Dr. Bell, " The glacial phenomena of the drift period in these latitudes correspond, in every way, with what may be observed on a small scale in connection with modern glaciers and there can be no doubt that they are due to land ice.

The striæl on rock surfaces were, it is conjectured, not all produced at the same time, but by different glaciers. As the great mass moved on, it became divided into smaller bergs, which would follow the valleys or be guided by their sides. The region of the Georgian Bay, as one of the great mineral depositaries of Ontario is, and will continue to be, of increasing interest and importance. A railway is proposed to be constructed from the mouth of the French River to Whitefish Station on the Canada Pacific road. This project has a very considerable bearing on the mining and lumbering interests and will do much for their development. Whitefish was formerly an important Hudson Bay Company post.

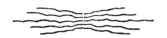

Evening Augusta

CHAPTER IV.

NATIVE INHABITANTS ; THE ASSIKINACKS AND OTHER
DISTINGUISHED CHIEFS AND WARRIORS.

HE Charter under which the Indians of the Province enjoy their rights, is the royal proclamation issued by King George III, in 1763, after the Treaty of Paris. Trespassing on their lands, and purchasing of them by the king's other subjects, were thereby forbidden. Indian lands were only to be purchased for the public use, at public meetings of the Indians to be held for that purpose by the Governor of the Province. The Quebec Act of 1774, and the Constitutional Act, forming the Dominion in 1867, contained similar provisions. The care of the Indians, and their reserved lands, is now vested in the Dominion Government.

The object of the Crown, as explained in the

(63)

instructions by the Colonial Minister, Lord Glenelg, to Sir F. B. Head, when Governor in 1838, was to segregate the red from the white population until the former were, by education and paternal care, raised to a level and made able to compete with the latter. "The first step to the real improvement of the Indians," says Lord Glenelg, "is to gain them over from a wandering to a settled life, and for this purpose it is essential that they should have a sense of permanency in the locations assigned to them, that they should be attached to the soil by being taught to regard it as reserved for them and their children, by the strongest securities." Before the appropriation of reserves, the Indians have no claim, except upon the bounty and benevolence of the Crown. After the appropriation, they become invested with a recognized tenure of land. They are wards of the State under pupilage. They have the advantages and safe guards of private citizens, having the present right to the exclusive usufruct, and a potential right to become individual owners in fee after enfranchisement. Such part of their ancestral estate as is not required for reserves, is generally sold, as demand arises, under treaty arrangements, by the Government and the interest derived from investment of the proceeds is annually divided among the members of the various bands entitled. (*a*)

(*a*) The Five Nation Indians, Iroquois, are specially referred to in the Treaty of Utrecht sec. xv. See also the St. Catharines Milling Company v. The Queen, Ontario Law Reports, vol. 10, and Appeal Cases, Law Reports vol. 14, 45 ; Houston's Constitutional Documents 72.

The paternal care and fairness exercised by the officers under Royal and Canadian authority, in the conduct of their affairs, have almost uniformly secured the good will of the aborigines, and have saved our soil from the horrors of Indian massacres from which our Southern neighbors have often suffered. On Grand Manitoulin Island, and at Cape Croker, are large settlements of civilized Indians, some of whom we met. The Chippewas, otherwise known as Ojibewas, and the Ottawas, of Lake Huron and the Georgian Bay, are divided into fifteen bands, settled on as many reserves on the shores of the lake and bay. Most of them are Christians in faith with here and there a pagan family. When meeting the whites, they are generally reserved and reticent. We had evidence of their taciturnity towards strangers, when approaching Killarney in the dark, and seeking the channel, we hailed some Indian vessels, using English and French, and finally our best Chippewa, but not a word would they reply to our call of "*Friend! Amis!*" or "*Bo' jou' Nitsi!*" There is probably no region where folk-lore and old tales, of war and romance, more abound than in the isles and on the shores of the Georgian Bay. The ancient customs are not forgotten and beneath every dark skin, though clad in "store clothes," there is a remnant of inbred and inherited superstition, which is exhibited at certain seasons to a marked degree. Many of them assembled this summer at the Shawanaga Reserve, on the east side of the bay to attend a war dance. Even after interment with Christian burial rites, the grave is often at night strewn with blankets, tin cups, pots, kettles, bowls, spoons and bits of cloth, articles which, according to their old superstition, would be useful to the shades in the spirit world. The Algic Manito is thus slow to give way before the white man's Theos.

The Grand Manitoulin Island is through tradition, believed to be the dwelling place of both the Good Spirit, Gitci Manito, and of Matci Manito, the Evil One. At a chosen time each summer, the different Indian bands of the Georgian Bay and Lake Huron, meet at a selected spot on this island to " shoot the Evil Spirit." After performing some wild and fantastic dances, with much howling and contortions, each man seizes his gun and a simultaneous volley is discharged, with great shouting. Festivities follow, sometimes ending in noisy orgies, for these red men are not all teetotalers. The following extract from the report of the late Right Hon. Sir John A. Macdonald, Superintendent of Indian Affairs, dated 1st January, 1886, will be of interest for its condensed information : " There are six day schools on Manitoulin Island and five on the mainland. The Indians of Manitoulin Island keep the roads, running through their reserves, in good order. This is especially the case on the Wikwemikong Reserve. The Indian population of the Superintendency of Northern Ontario is 3,343. They hold 3,120 acres under cultivation. Their crops amounted in the aggregate to 4,269 bushels and 1,290 tons of hay. The fish captured by them were valued at \$18,450, and the furs at \$5,205.50, while the revenue derived from the other industries is estimated to have amounted to \$5,850." By arrangement with the Government, the Indians of the eastern part of Manitoulin have also, during 1889 and since, cut a large amount of merchantable timber.

The land of the Hurons or Wyandots, lay between the Georgian Bay and Lake Simcoe. It was a beautiful heritage with favoured surroundings, pure water, fertile soil, game and fish in abundance.

This region is a prolific field for the work of the archeologist. When single graves are opened, the skeleton is often found in a sitting posture, objects in bone, shell, stone, copper and pottery are laid beside it. The burial places were generally great ossuaries, pits, containing the remains of from a hundred to several thousand bodies. While burial sometimes took place in single graves, the usual custom was, as each Indian died, to place the body on a stage raised above the reach of wild animals. At periods of some years, fixed at solemn councils, the remains were taken down simultaneously, the shreds of flesh were carefully removed, large pits were made and into these all the bones were cast with much wailing and noisy ceremony. These ossuaries are easily found, the surface falling in as the decaying bones cease to support it. Many of them have been opened, and specimens from them, generally skulls, grace the collections of various museums. It has been usually thought that the burial of articles with the dead was a religious act. If it were, then the custom would doubtless seldom have been omitted, but in many of the graves no such articles are found, and of the ossuaries, one may contain a thousand articles, and another scarcely a pipe or bead.

Mr. C. A. Hirschfelder, who is well known as an archeologist, says as to this, " We know that the Indians lived up to their belief, and if it had been an act of religion to thus bury articles, then in each and every grave some article would be found. . . . My theory is this, if one of these ' feasts of the dead ' should occur during a propitious season, many articles could be spared, but if a famine stared the Indians in the face, which frequently happened, they would be too poor to spare articles, and it appears to me that the act of burial was not one of religion, but one of respect." This opinion is not entirely acquiesed in by other authorities. The truth probably is that the rite of leaving gifts with the dead arose both from affection and superstition.

The Chippewas and Ottawas were not much concerned with the internecine strife between the Iroquois and Hurons of two hundred and fifty years ago. They then resided to the west of the Huron territory. As the Hurons and their relations of the Neutral and Tobacco nations, who held the territory south of the Bay as far as Lake Ontario, and along the north shore of Lake Erie, were driven out of their lands, the ancestors of the present possessors came in and gradually occupied it, the Mohawks and other Iroquois re-

maining in more southern regions. The Ottawas had
specially chosen Manitoulin Island, and the North
Shore and Channel, as the seat of their nation, and
jealously guarded them from Mohawk incursions and
encroachment. The Ottawas had at one time set up
their tepees along the waters of the Upper Ottawa as
far as Allumette Island, and the site of the present
large town of Prescott, but had not attempted long to
hold that disputed territory.

These people live in a tribal way, the regulation of
their affairs is in the hands of councils chosen by themselves. The oldest system of government on the continent is in practical operation in their council-houses.
Their code of rules and regulations, when adopted
and approved by the Governor-General of Canada in
Council, forms an excellent quasi-municipal system,
including the management of roads, fences, ditches,
schools and pounds. They generally exhibit much
interest in educational matters.

As any one may desire, there is legal provision for
him, with the consent of the Superintendent of Indian Affairs, to leave his band and become enfranchised, when he takes the status of a white man with
the like privileges and obligations. This right was,
until recent years, rarely sought, but since the date of
the incident about to be related, Indian men in the
older provinces have had the electoral franchise extended to them on like terms as enjoyed by their
white neighbours.

Mr. S. J. Dawson, for some years member of

Parliament for Algoma, relates that, when canvassing
or votes at West Bay on the Grand Manitoulin, he
accosted a well-known Indian who was a fur trader
and had a general store, and asked for his vote. "Do
you not know that I am a member of my band," he
replied. "But why not be enfranchised? with all
your means you surely do not value the dole you
receive from government!" "It is not that," said the
native patriot, "all I so receive is $8 a year. In that
building is, I think, $10,000 worth of goods, but I
would rather give all that than abandon the position
I occupy among my people, or take any step that
would separate me, in the least degree, from them."
It is from the residents along these shores, of pure
and mixed blood, that many of the hardy voyageurs,
raftsmen and axemen in lumber camps, or engaged in
moving the great tows of logs, covering many acres
in extent, are gathered. They are a jovial and hardy
race. They are among the bravest hunters and
fishermen. The old French blood mingles in the
veins of not a few of those occupying these northerly
settlements. Many of the families have become
known for their sterling character and independent
circumstances. They have interests in valuable mines,
some of which were discovered or developed by
their heads, or are well to do traders with extensive
business ramifications throughout the wilder country
to the north and west. Their young people are
educated at the schools at Wikwemikong and elsewhere in the district, and at the Shingwauk and

Wawonosh Homes near Ste. Marie, and there are
Metes ladies who have taken courses of music and
French in Toronto, Montreal or Paris.   Among such
families the names of Sawyer, Corbeau, Biron and
D'Lamorondiere are prominent.   As to the Indians
living in tribal manner—if happiness is to be secured ,
by possessing a sufficiency, freedom from rent or
taxes, and from action in any civil court, all of which
these wards of the Dominion enjoy, then they may
be considered signally favored.

On inquiry as to how this legal protection acted
on the character, we were told by white merchants,
that while many of the Indians honorably make good
their engagements, some can not be trusted, and
bargains can only be safely conducted with them on
a cash basis.   The strict honesty found by Henry, the
old fur trader, among their ancestors, is not so general
now.   He relates that he had the satisfaction of
seeing all those to whom he had advanced the price
of peltries return, not thirty skins remained unpaid,
and this trivial deficit was occasioned by the death of
one of the Indians, for whom his family offered to
make good the loss, fearing that until that was done
his spirit would not rest. (a)

In the neighborhood of the Georgian Bay Reserves
wild animals abound, the moose and red deer, black
bears, foxes, beavers, water fowl, partridge or grouse.
The dread rattlesnake and copper-head disappear
when the pig is introduced.   There is much excellent

(a) **Henry's Travels, part 1, cap. v.**

soil on the Grand Manitoulin. In addition to the
farms tilled by the Indians, are many occupied by
white residents in the neighborhood of the main
settlements, Little Current, Gore Bay, Mudge Bay and
Manitowaning. Shegwiandah is also an important
and beautiful village. Hardwood is found as well as
the pine, poplar, spruce and hemlock, nor do we see
on the shore the destruction by fire, leaving the rocks
bare and black, so common in the more frequented
region of Muskoka.

KEEJEK AND ASSIKINACK—INDIAN LIFE AND TRADITIONS.

> Ye who love the haunts of nature,
> Love the sunshine of the meadow,
> Love the shadow of the forest,
> Love the wind among the branches,
> And the rain-shower and the snow-storm,
> And the rushing of great rivers,
> Through their palisades of pine-trees
> And the thunder in the mountains,
> Whose innumerable echoes
> Flap like eagles in their eyries ;
> Listen to these wild traditions.
>
> —*Song of Hiawatha.*

Two young men of one of the tribes, still represented by the Indians of the Georgian Bay, became
favorably known to many in Toronto more than fifty
years ago. Charles Tebisco Keejek entered Upper
Canada College, where he developed much skill as a
linguist, and was well thought of by those who knew
him. He aided the late Rev. Canon O'Meara, in
translating the New Testament into Chippewa. Mr.

O'Meara was then a missionary to the Indians of the
Grand Manitoulin. Keejek settled at the Indian
village of Wobonash, near Owen Sound, where he
cultivated a small farm, and, by writing and otherwise, gave much attention to the affairs of his tribe.
He also for a time acted as interpreter to the Rev. R.
Robinson, Congregational missionary. He was an
excellent scholar, retiring in manner and of finely cut
features. He married a woman of his people and died
at Wobonash more than twenty years ago, leaving an
intelligent and industrious family.

Francis Assikinack, the other lad, also held high
place in his classes; was on the prize list in 1841 for
good conduct and map-drawing, and in 1843 was first
form boy and first in writing, general proficiency,
Greek and geography. He was son of a Chief who
lived to a great age and who was present at the taking
of Macinac on the eastern shore of Michigan, four hundred miles north of Detroit. It was sometimes called
Fort Michilli-Mackinack, meaning the Great Turtle,
when a boy, on the 2nd of June, 1763, in the Pontiac
war. It was then that a hord of Sacs and Chippewa
Indians gathered round the fort in friendly disguise,
but their sympathies were with the French. Under
pretence of a game of baggataway, or lacrosse, they
induced the unwary garrison to come, as spectators,
beyond the palisades, seized the weapons, which the
squaws had meantime concealed under their blankets,
and then ensued a bloody massacre of officers and men.
Assikinack was then too young to take an active

5

part in this affair, nor did his tribe do so, though they, the Ottawas, were in the neighborhood. (a)

Assikinack and his friend,Thomas George Anderson, were again at Macinac when Fort Holmes, as the citadel was named, was taken by Captain Roberts, early in the war of 1812.

On the prairie, now included in the State of Illinois, was a stockade,-built in 1685 by Durantaye, and in 1804 occupied by a small American garrison. It was called Fort Dearborn in honor of the General of that name. Father Marquette had been there in 1674 and planted a mission station. It was in the path of the explorer. La Salle and Charlevoix visited it. In 1796, Jean Baptiste du Sable, a colored man, settled on the banks of the skunk-infested stream which cut its way past the military post in the prairie down to Lake Michigan. The Indians used to say that "the first white settler was a negro." Then a Canadian, John Kinzie, from Quebec, opened trade here, and was for twenty years the only white resident beyond the limits of the fort.

After Macinac was taken, Assikinack appeared as the leader of a company of Ottawa and Pottawatomie Indians, at Fort Dearborn. He was already known to General Harrison and other American authorities, and his name had been introduced into historical documents relating to Indian affairs, as " The Black-Bird," and sometimes as " The Black-Partridge."

(a) Pontiac was principal chief of the Ottawas.   Tecumseh adopted him as his model.   The action of June, 1763, is described in Parkman's "Conspiracy of Pontiac," Vol. I., p. 276; also in Henry's Travels, Part I., ch. ix.

Captain Heald was in charge of Fort Dearborn in 1812. To him Assikinack went and returned a silver medal he had received from his Government, saying he was unable to restrain his young warriors, and being compelled to act as an enemy, he could no longer wear the token of friendship. On the 15th of August the garrison evacuated the place, but did not escape an unfortunate attack from the Indians, who were angered because of a breach in the conditions of surrender, the soldiers having destroyed part of the ammunition and arms which they had agreed to leave intact. Assikinack warned them of their danger. He went to the interpreter, Mr. Griffith, and said, in his own tongue and manner: "Linden birds have been singing in my ears to-day; be careful on the march you are going to take." He restrained the Pottawatomies and Ottawas with him, in as far as was in his power. He personally saved Mrs. Helm, step-daughter of Mr. Kinzie, from the scalping-knife. On the site of this post is now the proud city of Chicago. The place of conflict with the savages and where the Americans surrendered to Assikinack, is about fifty yards from the lake shore, south of North street, and between Indiana and Michigan avenues.

The medal referred to was given to ' Black-Bird ' at the treaty of Fort Wayne, made by General Harrison on the 30th September, 1809. An engraving of it, the size of the original, is given at page 306 of Lossing's Pictorial History of the War of 1812. On one side is the bust of President Madison, surrounded with the words " James Madison, President of the U. S. 1809." On the reverse two hands are clasped ; there are also a tomahawk and pipe, and the motto, "Peace and Friendship." It is entitled "The Black Partridge's Medal." There was a distinguished Mandan Indian Chief called Black-Bird, who died about the beginning of this century. Dressed in warlike paraphernalia, and placed on his favorite white steed, the dead chief and living horse were buried together on the banks of the Missouri river. (*a*)

Our Ottawa chief is not to be confounded with him. The Department of the Interior at Washington has kindly furnished the writer with a copy of the record of a conference between President Madison and an Indian delegation, dated Washington, 5th October, 1811. The Ottawa Nation is there represented by " Black-Bird or Siginoc, Chief of the Ottawa Delegation." Much complaint is set out of breach of promises made by American Indian Commissioners, and yet it is alleged peace had been maintained and the efforts of the Prophet, brother of Tecumseh, are referred to as of " one who has frequently endeavoured to stir up a hostile disposition in our minds towards the American people, but our ears are closed to these bad birds which sing around us, and we have returned for answer that whoever listened to the advice of the Prophet or his followers would be destroyed by the American people." (*b*) Black-Bird was active during

(*a*) Geo. Catlin's Travels, vol. 2, 5.
(*b*) For the treaties referred to see U. S. Statutes at large. vol. 7, pp. 113-115, and Am. State Papers, Indian Affairs, vol. 1, p. 761. See also Appendix to this chapter.

all the time of this war harassing the enemy at Niagara and elsewhere.

We find him attached to Captain Worsley's Company in September, 1814, when that officer found it necessary to scuttle his schooner, the *Nancy*, at the mouth of the Nottawasaga, where we believe her hull still lies, he at once took canoes and passed through Lake Huron to Macinac. Here he found the port blockaded by Commodore Sinclair with two armed American schooners. These were gallantly boarded and taken. *(a)*

Assikinack, who is called 'Sackanaugh,' was observed just before the attack, with tobacco pouch and bottle of rum, scattering part of their contents on the waters of the bay. This was with devotional feelings, and by way of invoking the "spirit of the waters." Then he rushed to the attack and was among the first to leap on board one of the enemy's vessels. "The action was crowned with success." This is all Morgan narrates. Young Assikinack was told by his father, that he, and a number of other Indians, boarded the vessel so noiselessly, that the crew, who were in the cabin, only learned of the attack when the war-whoop rang out, and finding themselves in the power of the red warriors, surrendered at discretion. The loss of the *Nancy* was further avenged by the taking of the American schooners the *Tigress* and *Scorpion* on the third and fifth of September, 1814, in the North Channel. Doubtless our

_(a)_ Morgan's Guide to Canada. Longman & Co., 1824.

red hero was at these events also, which were the more notable as both these vessels had been in the famous engagement under Commodore Perry and Captain Barclay in Lake Erie in September, 1812. Morgan states that 'Sackanaugh' was a nephew of Tecumseh, the famous Shawanoe warrior. If so, his blood was of right royal strain. In Mr. Charles Mair's beautiful drama, "Tecumseh," that heroic chief is the leading character. When he fell in battle after the destruction of Fort Malden, General Harrison then in command of the enemy, afterwards President of the United States, and grandfather of the late occupier of the White House, pronounces his eulogy :

> Sleep well, Tecumseh, in thy unknown grave,
> Thou mighty savage, resolute and brave !
> Thou, master and strong spirit of the woods,
> Unsheltered traveller in sad solitudes,
> Yearner o'er Wyandot and Cherokee,
> Couldst tell us now what hath been and shall be !

The venerable William McMurray, now Archdeacon and Rector of Niagara, was the first English Church missionary to the Indians of the north shore of Lakes Superior and Huron, having been appointed by Lieutenant-Governor Sir John Colborne, the late Lord Seaton, on the 2nd of August, 1832. His mission headquarters were at Sault Ste. Marie. In an interesting note, of date 15th October 1892, addressed to the writer, Dr. McMurray says : " I knew Assikinack. He was interpreter to the Government, both at Manitoulin Island and along the north shore as far as Penetanguishene. He was a noted man, and held a prominent position among the Indians. The last time I saw him was in the summer of 1837. Mrs. Jameson, the author cf 'Winter Studies and Summer Rambles,' paid us a visit at Sault Ste. Marie, and expressed a strong desire to see the Indians receiving their presents at the Manitoulin. Her wishes were complied with. Mrs. McMurray and myself accompanied her in a small boat to that island. On our voyage down to the island, which took four days, we discovered a vessel on her way to the Sault. We hailed her to ascertain the news, and were informed that the King had died and that Queen Victoria had ascended the throne. On hearing that, Mrs. Jameson exclaimed : 'Poor thing, she little knows the troubles of those who wear the crown!' On our arrival at the Manitoulin Island, we found the Indians gathered in large numbers from the surrounding country. Mr. Samuel Peters Jarvis, who at that time was the Indian Commissioner, had the Indians all assembled, and through the aid of his interpreter, Assikinack, who had before this become a convert and taken the Christian name of Jean Baptiste, their presents were given them. We parted with Mrs. Jameson there, and she returned to Toronto with Mr. Jarvis."

In the third volume of the book referred to, the talented authoress gives a delightful account of her visit at the Sault, and of those most interesting native ladies met there : Mrs. Schoolcraft and Mrs. McMurray, and their aged mother, Mrs. Johnson, who was Neengai the beautiful daughter of Waub Ojeeg, a famous Chippewa chief. The voyage to Manitowaning was made

in a small but compact and well-built boat.   The
course was in the narrow part of Lake Huron, between
St. Joseph's island and the mainland, and through the
North Channel to the east end of Manitoulin Island.
Thus they sailed, or rowed, past the mouths of the
Garden and Thesalon rivers; the Missisauga, which
has its source in the interior, 300 miles north of the
waters of the North Channel, and the Serpent river,
where now are the great Cook lumber mills, through
an archipelago of islands, all clad in summer costume,
and with beautiful vistas, and ever changing scenes.
They had four voyageurs, Masta, Content, LeBlanc
and Pierrott, " all Canadian voyageurs of the true
breed, that is, half-breed, showing the Indian blood
as strongly as the French." She was enchanted with
the variety and beauty surrounding her on the trip.

Writing of the young Queen, she says: " What a
fair heritage is this which has fallen to her! a land
young like herself, a land of hopes, and fair, most fair!
Does she know, does she care anything about it!
While hearts are beating warm for her and voices
bless her, and hands are stretched out towards her,
even from these wild lake shores!" They came on
the fourth day to a " beautiful basin." nearly an exact
circle, of about three miles in circumference; in the
centre lay a little wooded island, and all around the
shores rose sloping from the margin of the lake, like
an amphitheatre, covered with wigwams and lodges,
thick as they could stand amid intermingled trees,
and beyond there arose the tall pine forest, crowning

and enclosing the whole. Some hundred canoes were darting, hither and thither, on the waters, or gliding along the shores, and a beautiful schooner lay against the green bank. Mr. Jarvis, the Chief Superintendent of Indian Affairs, and Captain Anderson, the Agent, received the party. It was a very noted gathering of the wild bands which was witnessed here, and even yet remembered and referred to as an historical event. There were many chiefs of the Ottawas, Pottawatomies and Chippewas, whose prowess was known from Thunder Cape to the Ohio. Their medicine men, squaws and papooses were with them. Charles Keejek and Francis Assikinack, then lads of ten or twelve years, enjoyed the affair as only boys can.

Wesleyan missionaries and Roman Catholic priests mingled with their converts. Of the Chippewas, Aisence, the Little Clam, Wai-sow-win-de-bay, Yellowhead and Shingua-cose, were most distinguished. Two Ears, a famous Pottawatomie, was fantastically dressed and painted, two clusters of swansdown depending from each ear. Waub-Ojeeg, son of Wayish-Ky, was a splendid specimen of Chippewa manliness, six feet three inches in height, his dress rich and tasteful, a surtout of fine blue cloth, under which was a shirt of gay colors, his father's medal fastened on his breast. His scalping knife and pouch hung from a magnificent embroidered belt of wampum. His leggings were of scarlet, embroidered with rich bands, or garters depending to his ankles. Four eagle's wing feathers were placed in an embroidered band around his head, in proof of his martial prowess. He held a tomahawk in his hand. His fine features were almost femininely soft. Then followed the distribution of presents and an address by Mr. Jarvis, who explained that Governor Sir Francis Head, left Toronto intending to preside, but hearing on the way of the king's death, had found it necessary to return. Old As-si-Kinack, the Black Bird, was chief interpreter, translating the meaning of the Superintendent's address to the great assembly, raising his voice to a high pitch, and speaking with much oratorical emphasis. " He is, Mrs. Jameson states, the most celebrated orator of the Ottawa nation." She was told with pride that, on one occasion, he began a speech at sunrise which lasted without intermission till sunset. Mokomaunish, an Ottawa chief and Shinguacose the eloquent Christian Chippewa, made long speeches in reply, Shinguacose, the Small Pine, was father of Shingwauk from whom the "Shingwauk Home" at Sault Ste. Marie, an important Church of England Indian school, received its name. A flag on which the lion and beaver were worked, was given on the occasion, the Indians choosing the old Ottawa chief, Kish-Kenick, to receive it. Then followed canoe races, the light barks paddled by squaws only, with a man to steer, and a war dance, inimitably described by this talented brave woman. All went on with good humour, and even good order, in the midst of confusion. " We are twenty white people, with 3,700 of these wild creatures around us, and I never in my life felt

more security." Word was brought the Superintendent that a trader from Detroit, with a boat laden
with rum, lay concealed in a cove, ready to waylay
the Indians and barter his fire-water for their new
blankets, guns and trinkets. Mr. Jarvis detailed
Assikinack with a canoe full of stout men, who soon
boarded the intruder and threw his stock in trade of
" ickutewabu," to the fishes.

" The Black Bird is, she says, a Christian, and extre-
mely noted for his general good conduct and his
declared enmity to the dealers in fire-water." A few
years after Mrs. Jameson's visit, Mr. Longfellow spent
some time in the region of the upper lakes. He had
doubtless before this become familiar with the writ-
ings of Henry R. Schoolcraft, who was brother-in-law
of Rev. Dr. McMurray, and celebrated as the great
delineator of native life and character. His volume
of Algic, or Algonquin, Researches, was published in
1839. It is also stated that Mr. Longfellow met some
of our north shore chiefs, and bards, and had from
their mouths legends of the Chippewas, Ottawas and
Pottawatomies, as they smoked pipes of peace together.
All these were soon after embodied in the Song of
Hiawatha.

CHAPTER V.

INDIAN LIFE AND TRADITIONS CONTINUED, " CENSUS of 1867 AND 1891," SHINGUACOSE AND CAPTAIN ANDERSON.

" From the Forest and the prairie,
" From the great lakes of the Northland,
" From the land of the Ojibways,
" From the land of the Dacotahs."

THE scene of the poem is laid by this American patriotically among the Indians, chiefly Chippewas, of the south shore of Lake Superior, but the life described was that of those who met at the great gathering at Manitowaning. The legend of Hiawatha, or rather Taounyawatha, the God of the Waters (a) is a collection of the myths and folklore of the Indian demi-god called Manabozho by the Algonquins, including the Chippewas or Ojibways, Ottawas and Pottawatomies, and Hiawatha by the Iroquois. Schoolcraft states that

(a) Parkman Conspiracy of Pontiac, Vol. I, 12.

these stories were first related to him by the Chippewas of Lake Superior in 1822 (*a*). He was then Indian Agent at Michillimackinac. Manabozho was the embodiment of the Algic conscience and manly virtue. Whatever the wisest and strongest of men could do, he could do ; like Hercules, he rid the earth of monsters; his birth and parentage were mysterious, his grandmother was daughter of the moon, and his father was the west-wind.

Alexander Henry, in 1767, gave a version of some of the Manabozho legends. The Algic demi-god was called also Michabou, Messou, Shectac, Nanibojou and Nanibozho, and represented as the founder, and indeed creator, of the Indian nations of North America. His burial place is on an Island, called Nanibozho, on the eastern side of Michipocoton Bay on the north shore, and was held in reverence by the natives in Henry's day. " I landed, he says, and found on the projecting rocks, a quantity of tobacco, rotting in the rain, together with kettles, broken guns and a variety of other articles. His spirit is supposed to make this its constant residence, and here to preside over the lake, and over the Indians in their navigation and fishing. This island lies no farther from the main, than the distance of 500 yards." (*b*)

Such is the last resting place of the mythic Hiawatha, or Manabozho. It is on Canadian soil about 100 miles north-west from Sault Ste. Marie. The place

---

(*a*) Introduction to " Hiawatha Legends " by Schoolcraft.
(*b*) Henry's Travels, part 2, cap. iv.

is still held in veneration as the chosen burial place of the hero-god, whose name has for hundreds of years been a household word in the wigwams of our Canadian aborigines.

Longfellow claimed him as American in the same spirit that the late poet Laureate made the "foremost Captain of our time, England's greatest son," not deeming it necessary to state that the great Duke first opened his eyes at Dungan Castle in the Emerald Isle. (a) Canada may as certainly claim to have on her soil the grave of Hiawatha as can Ireland to contain the birth place of the conqueror of Napoleon.

In a late learned article by Rev. W. M. Beauchamp, the archeologist, on *Hiawatha*, he states, "When Longfellow's Hiawatha appeared, I was prepared to greet an old friend, and surprised at being introduced to an Ojibway instead of an Iroquois leader. The change however gave a broader field for his beautiful poem, a gain to all readers, but, as he retained little beyond the name, it may be needless to refer to that charming work." (b)

Ta-oun-ya-wat-ha, here called the "Holder of the Heavens," is distinguished in this article from Hiawatha, "the very wise man," who was an Onondaga Indian. Much attention has of late been given by other scholars to the study of folk-lore. The myths of the Ojibways, Missisaugas, Ottawas and other Algonquins have been so well collated and analyzed by A. F.

(a) Tennyson's Ode on the Death of Wellington.
(a) Journal of American Folk-lore, vol. iv. 295.

Chamberlain, Ph. D., that it is only necessary to refer to his published work. (*a*) From this we learn that a rock on the south-east shore of Michipocoton Bay marks where Manabozho rested after jumping across that piece of water. ·

On the north shore of the lake, eastward from Thunder Bay Point, is his grave, according to another legend given in the journal of the late Peter Jacobs. The name of Manabozho (or Nanibozhu) has also been given to a mountain overhanging the waters of Lake Superior and to a point of land close by. Near to that is stated to be a large impression resembling that left when a man sits down in the snow. Whenever the Indians pass by any of these places, they invariably drop some tobacco, so that Manabozho may smoke in his kingdom in the west. These are not to be confounded with the figure of the Manito seen from Port Arthur, as he lies in his long sleep, bold and grand, under the sky, forming the crest of Thunder Cape, three miles long and nearly one thousand feet above the lake. On a smooth rock on the shores of the Ottawa river, there are prints of human footsteps and near by a round hole, about the shape and size of a kettle. These the Ottawas and Chippawas believe to be the track of Manabozho and the kettle which he dropped. Into these tobacco is thrown as a luck offering.

Mr. John McIntyre, of Fort William, one of the oldest employes of the Hudson Bay Company, in-

(*a*) Ibid, 193.

forms me that a mountain in Black Bay, Lake Superior, is called Nanibozhu, and the Indians are never known to pass it without throwing in a piece of tobacco.

In Mr. Paul Kane's valuable book, "Wanderings of an Artist," an account is given of Manitowaning in 1845, as a village of forty or fifty log houses, built by the Provincial Government for the Indians, a mission with a church, a pastor, Indian agent, doctor and blacksmith, all paid by Government. Mr. Kane was an eminent painter, who spent several years among the Indians of the Canadian North-West. The Canadian Government purchased many of his pictures of Indian life, but most of these were unfortunately consumed by fire. Others, forming an interesting collection, are possessed by Senator Allan of Toronto. The artist found nearly two thousand Indians awaiting the arrival of the vessel freighted with their annual presents, comprising guns, ammunition, axes, kettles and other implements useful to the Indians. Assikinack, called here " Sigennok," was, Mr. Kane says, an acute and intelligent Indian, appointed to distribute to his tribe their due share of the presents annually consigned to them. He was styled Interpreter, though he could not speak English, but his natural eloquence was such that he possessed great influence over his tribe; "indeed," says Mr. Kane, "it is to the untiring volubility of his tongue that he owes his name, ' The Black Bird.' "

Captain Anderson, then Superintendent of Indian

Affairs, related to Mr. Kane a sad tale of Assikinack's
depravity in his younger days, through excessive
drinking. He was, when under such influence, a
maniac; only to be controlled by main force, which
was attended with danger owing to his Herculean
strength. His attendants therefore, when he was so
crazed, plied him with more spirits, until he sank into
insensibility. Captain Anderson found him once in
such besotted state, lying in front of his lodge in
drunken oblivion, and bound him hand and foot with
strong cords, placing a decrepid boy to watch near
him. When Assikinack awoke, he angrily demanded
of the boy, who had dared to treat him with such in-
dignity? The boy, without replying, called the captain, who coming told the chief that he had been
bound by the boy by his orders, and left exposed to
the derision of the camp, a shameful position for one
who pretended to be a leader of his people. Then followed a severe lecture on intemperance, which the
fettered warrior took so well to heart, that he promised to forever abandon his degrading habit. Captain Anderson then unbound him, and Assikinack is
said to have never been known to violate the promise
so made. He is also said to have used all his eloquence
in endeavours to persuade his people to renounce
heathenism for Christianity, and at a protracted council or meeting, to have spoken almost without ceasing
for three days. A gentleman, who met him at an
Indian Treaty gathering at Penetanguishene about
1856 found him still active and influential but much

6

bent and aged. He died on the second of November,
1866, at the age of 98 years, and was interred at
Wikwenikong, as we are informed by the Rev. D.
Duranquet of that mission.

Young Francis was a noble specimen of his race,
stood six feet one inch in his stockings, was of lithe
form, jet-black hair, somewhat aquiline nose, piercing
eye and had small and beautiful hands and feet.
He mastered languages with ease, and read history
with avidity.   He left college after entering the sixth
form, but continued his readings under the care of
Bishop Charbonnell, and some other cultivated French
clerics, then in Toronto, for he was a devoted Roman-
ist.   He carried from the college excellent testimonials
from the principal, Mr. Barron, and from Dr. McCaul.
His favorite pastime in winter was the making of
snow forts when, sides being taken by each boy, the
opposing forces attacked each other with snow balls,
not ceasing till the stronghold was taken.   In agility
and strength of body he distanced most competitors
but did not care for cricket or other games of ball.
Lacrosse had not then been introduced as a white boy's
game.   He shot a robin on the wing with his bow
and arrow and his aim with a rifle was unerring.   On
one occasion he ran a race in the Queen's Park with a
mounted English Officer and got to Queen Street in
a half mile run, before the galloping horse.   He was
employed in the Government Indian Department, his
appointment as clerk and interpreter being dated 10th
August, 1849, where his knowledge of languages and

of his people proved of service. When filling the office of interpreter to the Department, Assikinack, who styled himself "a warrior of the Odahwahs," read four able and critical papers before the Canadian Institute at Toronto. Three of these are in their journal of 1858, the first on "Legends and Traditions of Odahwah Indians," the second on their "Social and Warlike Customs" and the third, which is completed in the volume of 1860, on their language. The late lamented Sir Daniel Wilson, then editor of the journal, appended an editorial note to the first article in which Assikinack is stated to have been a fullblood Odahwah or Ottawa Indian, sent to the college by Mr. Samuel P. Jarvis, Superintendent General of Indian Affairs in 1840, when totally ignorant of the English language. In style of composition the articles referred to are clear and eloquent and seem modeled after Macaulay's historical essays. The proper name of his nation was Odahwah, as given, but he submits to variation into *Ottawa,* by which it is now generally known. His discussion of the nomenclature of the numerous tribes of this nation, their customs "Ododams" or coats of arms, their councils, marriage and funeral-rites, feasts, modes of government, religion, legends and myths are original and most interesting. Among the last, are those of the creation of men from "mere animals walking on four feet, mute, filthy, acorn-eating savages, until, from constant fighting, scratching and what-not, they learned to stand erect and walk upon their feet." The flood with Manahbozho for Noah, is a longer

story. This demi-god is of course the same as Manabozho or Hiawatha, but Assikinack does not refer to
Mr. Longfellow's poem, then published for some time.
We are given to understand that he did not regard it
as an entirely accurate representation of the characteristics of his race. He felt perhaps some jealousy or
pique, as a warrior of the Odahwahs, because of the
author giving his hero the Iroquois appellation, instead of his native Algonquin, Manabozho, thus hon-
oring a nation which had been at enmity with his
own from time immemorial, and whom he regarded
as but interlopers or trespassers on the north shore.
In the myth, as related by Assikinack, Manabozho
made of a piece of mud a large island which he placed
in the agitated waters where it continued to increase
until it formed the earth, as it is now. He continued
to reside with men some time after the flood, instruct-
ing them in the use of many things necessary for
their well-being. " He then told them that he was
going away from them ; that he would fix his permanent residence in the north, and that he would never
cease to take deep interest in their welfare. As a
proof of his regard for mankind, he assured them
that he would, from time to time, raise a large fire,
the reflection of which would be visible to them.
Hence the northern lights are regarded by the Indians
as the reflection of the great fire, kindled occasionally
for the purpose of reminding them of the assurance
made of old by their benefactor. Another legend
was, that the tribes were one and the same people at

the beginning. Then great disputes arose, as to the
foot of a bear which was a favorite Algonquin viand,
second only to roast puppy, and when they could not
make up their differences, they quietly dispersed in
various directions, and their children became distinct
nations under different names. A myth heard by him
in childhood was, he thought possibly a tradition or
Indian account, of the rescue of the Israelites and the
drowning of the Egyptians, by the waters of the Red
Sea. It is usually told, he said, as follows: "Several
brothers, or a body of men of the tribe, were pur-
sued and hard pressed by fierce enemies, and being
driven to the end of the earth. When it was impossible for them to retreat any further, one of them
suddenly turned round and struck the earth with his
stick, which immediately opening, all their pursuers
were swallowed up in the yawning abyss, the earth
closed again, and thus he saved his companions and
himself from death."

Assikinack expressed the opinion that his remote
ancestors entered America from Asia through what is
known as Russian America. Referring to the name of
his village, Manitowaning, in the great island of the bay,
he shewed that the Odahwah word for god was Manido
or Mahnido, the personation of terror and irresis-
table power. He called attention to the remarkable
circumstance that the Seiks of Hindostan, and other
Hindoos, call their supreme God Mahadeo when viewed
in the light of Destroyer, that these words, *Mahnido*
and *Mahadeo*, should resemble each other in sound

and in signification, was, he reasoned, not altogether
the work of chance. The remainder of the word,
waning, means hollow or cave. There is a part of the
adjacent bay in which the Indians say they could
never find bottom by their longest trolling lines. From
this circumstance that spot in the bay received the
name Manitowaning. On this island his ancestors
were settled when Columbus first sighted the Western
World, 'from this they sent a party of warriors to
Montreal, on learning of the arrival of the French
there. When the party returned their canoes were
laden with strange articles which they had received
from the Wamitikgooshe, as they called the foreigners,
from the fact that they kept their goods in boxes of
wood, as that word implies. There was a sad romance
in his life. He became engaged to an English lady of
culture and position. Then he fell ill and consulted
a physician, who found him suffering from decline,
and could not entirely conceal his anxiety, yet feared
to speak the truth. The young Assikinack sought a
friend and begged him to learn all. To him the doctor said, " Yes, the Indian will die." On meeting him,
Assikinack read his fate in his friend's sad face and
said : " I see my friend I must die." Then he man-
fully put his affairs in order, wrote a touching farewell to the lady whom he had hoped soon to be his
bride, obtained leave of absence from his office, and
went home to his people on the Isle of the Manito.
As he discussed his sad fate with his Toronto friends
he said : " There is a beautiful maple grove in my

people's old camping ground, I will put up a wigwam and end my days there." Soon a white marble slab at Wikwomikong marked, as it still does, his last resting place. He died on the 21st November, 1863. The township, in which the village is situate has been given his tribal name Assikinack. Romance is often said to form no part of the Indian character, but we know how chivalrous, as also how cruel, the warrior could be. Assikinack would sometimes refer in sadness to the decadence of the Spartan character, and the vices which were destroying his race. Of their oratory he once said : " There were good speakers among the Indians formerly, but I have too much reason to believe that there are no such speakers to be found among them at the present day. In my opinion it was chiefly owing to their deep contemplation in their silent retreats in the days of youth, that the old Indian orators acquired the habit of carefully arranging their thoughts; when, instead of the shoutings of drunken companions, they listened to the warbling of birds, whilst the grandeur and the beauties of the forest, the majestic clouds, which appear like mountains of granite floating in the air, the golden tints of a summer evening sky, and all the changes of nature, which then possessed a mysterious significance, combined to furnish ample matter for reflection to the contemplating youth."

He would also relate to his friends, with earnestness and flashing eye, the valorous traditions of his race. He was the youngest son of his father's third wife. Late in life the old man, blind with age, told his boy many incidents of Ottawa and Iroquois conflicts. It was a tradition of his nation that they had, hundreds of years ago, come from the south-west ascending by the Mississippi and its tributaries. — Representatives of both the Ottawas and Chippewas occupy the reserves of the Georgian Bay in peaceful pursuits. Yet they were slowly disappearing and fading away, and this was more apparent in his day than now. Discussing this with young Assikinack, once in Toronto, he answered, "Yes, we are going it is true, and when we are gone our deeds will still fill pages in the white man's history. We have in Canada mingled in his wars, first against him, then with him, against the common enemy."

Desirous of learning the facts as to the prospects of the Indians under Government care in the older Provinces, inquiry made of the Minister having Indian affairs under his charge has elicited the valuable table giving the relative numbers in 1867 aud 1891 in Ontario and Quebec, shewing a gratifying result. This table is appended.

Being in a communicative mood, speaking of the Mohawks, and of the slaughter of the Hurons, young Assikinack said, "They were great warriors, and masters of the art of war, as they understood it. They drove the Hurons systematically from the lakes and from Canada West. They attacked the French and Hurons at La Prarie, within sight of fortified Montreal. They plundered the great warehouses and burned their victims before the eyes of the inhabitants and garrison, and left as quietly as they came, for their homes in the old province of New York." He probably referred to the invasions of the Five Nations in 1689.

There is, he said, a legend I learned from my father of an affair between the Odahwahs and the Mohawks, which took place near where a town is now being laid out on the Georgian Bay, and a railway built from Toronto. It is a high piece of land, having a good outlook eastward and westward. The Mohawks and other Iroquois, to the number of one hundred or more, were here encamped. They used to come north, to the vicinity of the Blue Mountains, by the Nahdowa-Sahgi river, now called the Nottawasaga. The Odahwahs occupying the Manitoulin and Saugeen Peninsula, resented their encroachments. Sahgimah, their great warrior chief, found the Mohawks on this high land called then, and by the Indians to this day, Sahgimah's watching place. He spied out their camp and found them feasting and dancing, suspecting no danger. He then gave his men orders to be ready. After night fell, he entered the camp alone and removed the arms, the short stiff bows, and the guns of the sleeping warriors. The Odahwahs then crept through the woods and in canoes, in shadow and darkness, along the coast, and gained the highland at midnight. The Mohawks were sleeping in circles round their extinguished camp fires. Behind each warrior was his property

pole, on which, in a buckskin bag, hung his pemmican
and other effects.   The war-whoop rang out over the
beautiful bay, and was echoed back from cliff to
island, when the Mohawks found themselves before
a foe remorseless as panthers.   A few only escaped.
The heads of the slain were cut off and fixed, each on
his property pole, with ghastly faces toward the lake,
in a mocking watch of horror.   Sahgimah then
loaded a canoe with provisions and ammunition, and
giving it to the captives, ordered them to go home
and never to return and to tell their people that
Sahgimah held watch on the Blue Mountains, and
would place the head of every Mohawk who would
there intrude, on his pole with face turned toward the
lake.   The site of this massacre was, as Assikinack
understood from his father, on the high land overlooking the Georgian Bay, a little west of the present
town of Collingwood.

Francis Assikinack was an interested student of the
late war between the Northern and Southern States.
When the fighting approached the old battle-grounds,
where his forefathers had contended, his martial
spirit was intensely aroused.   More than this, he
seemed to have inherited something of the power of
his famous grand uncle, the Prophet, brother of
Tecumseh.   On the morning of the seventeenth of
September, 1862, he said to a friend in his office:
"There is trouble somewhere, there is a great battle
going on. I feel it in the air."   Soon the telegraph
announced the terrible conflict at Antietam, between

the forces under McClellan and Lee. Had he lived in earlier days he would, no doubt, have been a noted leader of his race. In the few years passed among white people, his ability, industry and amiable character won him many friends, and proved him fitted to take an equal place with men of refinement. It has been a pleasure to his few surviving friends, who aided in collecting particulars of his career, thus to keep his memory green, as it is to the writer to make known some of his excellent qualities and the manner of his end, at once so sad and so characteristic of his heroic race.

The school record of Keejek, whose name signifies the sky, and of Assikinack is given from reference to the college register by the present Principal, George Dickson, M.A. He infers that Assikinack was the cleverer of the two. The names appearing on the class lists with these boys are of such men as Adam Crooks, who lived to be a distinguished lawyer and statesman; J. J. Kingsmill, a judge ; Norman Bethune, an eminent physician, and William Wedd, M.A. the classical scholar.

CHAPTER VI.

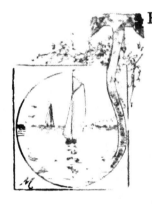

HE following account of pioneer shipping on the Georgian Bay is given by Mr. A. C. Osborne, of North Bay. Two vessels, the *Nawash* and *Tecumseth*, were built at Chippewa in 1818 and were brought to Penetanguishene in 1819. The next year Dr. Tarte, first military surgeon, was buried on Magazine Island which is opposite the present Juvenile Reformatory. The dock-yard was built that year. Two side-wheel steamers and one sloop-rigged vessel were built in the years 1821, '22, and '23. They were named respectively *Experiment Minos* and *Bull-Frog*. The last was commanded by Commodore Wooden. Each of these crafts was supplied with one cannon and manned by royal navy seamen. The *Wanderer* was afterwards brought over from Nottawasaga by Jeffery to carry stone

Lake Huron — near Wilderness
Meriwether, August 6, '83

104 GP

for the barracks. The *Water-Witch* also came from Nottawasaga or Macinac, having been taken from the Americans. Her exact history is not known. She, with the *Nawash* and *Tecumseth*, are sunk in the harbour of Penetanguishene. The other vessels were taken out of commission and dismantled. In 1822 Lieutenant, afterwards Admiral Bayfield, commenced the survey of Lake Huron in a vessel called the *Recovery*, furnished by the Government. It is not known where she was built. The *New Recovery* was built at Fort William in 1825, and furnished with two weeks' provisions to continue the survey of Lake Superior. The old Magazine was built at Penetanguishene in 1826-27. Its remains are still on Magazine Island. Mr. Osborne procured the above information from Mr. John Cowan, who was born in 1806 and died in 1892, in the Township of Tiny and who was with Admiral Bayfield from 1822 to 1825 inclusive. Mr. Cowan assisted Admiral Bayfield in building the *New Recovery* at Fort William and in launching and rigging her. " What became of the vessel ultimately I have," says Mr. Osborne, " no means of knowing. Mr. William Fraser tells me he frequently saw the *Minos* and *Experiment* pass up the Wye River past old Fort Ste. Marie, and into Mud Lake. This was years before the bridge over the river was built."

In winter the Georgian Bay is locked in ice, from two to three feet in thickness. It may be imagined that its aspect would then be dreary. But one who has often traversed its surface, in winter, on snow shoes, as well as in canoes in summer, affirms that such is not always the case. The margin of the bay, and the islands, produce a relieving back-ground of evergreens. The maples, elms, ashes, and other deciduous trees, show their bare trunks. The colors of the rocky sides, where the snow has no hold, reveal the syenitic red, and silurean and granitic grey, and the darker traps. The thousands of islands, which fringe the north-shore, for many miles, are blended in the view of the coast line. The light snow upon the ice is driven in all directions, under a clear sky. Then clouds of frozen vapour reflecting the sun's rays produce novel effects, as they are whirled upwards, and then onwards, on their courses, by the currents of air. Watched from the window of a cosy homestead, or from an eminence, they afford subject-matter for contemplation and admiration. It must not be assumed that the waters beneath the white blanketing, are motionless. The currents move in their courses as they did in summer, with the variation caused by protection from the direct action of the wind on the bay itself. The currents from the many rivers are soon lost in the mass with which they mingle, but the winds upon Lake Huron blow up the waters into this bay, and the lesser bays are affected by the pressure caused by these greater currents. A south-west wind will force the warmer and deeper waters of the lake through the sixteen mile entrance, between Cape Hurd on the Saugeen Peninsula, and the Grand Manitoulin, and thence it will pass along the north-shore to the head of the bay, when, meeting currents from the North-Channel and rivers, it will be distributed towards the centre. The waters beneath the ice are thus always in motion and of varying temperatures. This uneasiness of the water, in connection with the wind pressure from above and expansion, causes the ice to crack and to overlap, and force itself on points and islands. Hence long seams appear from headland to headland, most dangerous to teamsters and snow-shoers.

In April the bay is clear of ice; the woods give up their snow, the gulls return and the fields again assume their verdure. Warm May brings out the vegetation in its early summer dress. The birds have come back, the humming-bird is preparing for household duties, in sunny coves, and insect life is every where active.

When the United Empire Loyalists emigrated from the revolted colonies, now the United States, Canada was held to be a northern Siberia, but the peach stone was planted and the tree fruited. The region they had come to, proved to be equal to that they had abandoned. Now we know that our Great North-West is the natural home of the wheat plant, and also excels in root crops. The finest fruit is raised on the south shore of this bay. Apples of delicate flavour and free from blemish, have been produced at Sault Ste. Marie, at the west end of the North Channel. In a few years as good will be raised at the

head of the Nipissing, 100 miles north of Owen
Sound. Potatoes are ripe on the first of July on the
Manitoulins. On the south shore of James' Bay, the
Windsor bean flourishes in perfection. At Temiscamingue, 150 miles north of the Georgian Bay, maize,
potatoes, barley and oats are produced, all of fine
quality. Much climatic influence is to be attributed
to the heat-preserving power of the inland lakes,
which tempers the cool night air. The Georgian Bay
is, as will be seen, south of the latitudinal centre of
Ontario. The fact is established, that with proper
cultivation, including drainage, farming can be carried on with good results, in the enormous fertile
area south, east and west, of James' Bay. The day
will come when cattle, root-crops, barley and other
grains will be largely produced and exported from
that country. *(a)*

The white fish and salmon trout of the Georgian
Bay are highly esteemed and the business carried on,
in the taking of them and other fish, is extensive.
"There are more than 2,000 miles of nets in the
Georgian Bay and Lake Huron," said an intelligent
fisherman of the Minks. His estimate was not
thought extravagant by his fellow craftsmen.

Mrs. Jameson in her " Winter Studies and Summer
Rambles in Canada," refers with enthusiasm to the
whitefish of the upper lakes. " I declare to you that

(a) See Evidence of J. C. Bailey, C. E., and others in the
Report of the Royal Mineral Commission, Ontario, 1890 ; also the
Ontario Government pamphlets on "The Algoma District," 1878.
The Report of Wm. Ogilvie, P. L. S., to Minister of Interior, on
Peace River Country, 7th April, 1892.

I never tasted anything of the fish kind half so exquisite. If the Roman Apicius had lived in these latter days, he would certainly have made a voyage up Lake Huron to breakfast on the white fish of St. Mary's River, and would not have returned in dudgeon, as he did from the coast of Africa." "It is really," she says again, "the most luxurious delicacy that swims the waters." And she speaks of the enormous quantities caught here, and in bays and creeks around Lake Superior, " Besides subsisting the inhabitants, not less than eight thousand barrels were shipped last year." Her visit was in 1837, and at that time the business had not assumed the important proportions which it has now attained.

We have the evidence of Alexander Henry given 130 years ago to the like effect (a). " The whitefish, which exceed the trout as a delicious and nutritive fish, are here in astonishing numbers. In shape they somewhat resemble the shad. Those who live on them for months together preserve their relish to the end."

Let us inquire as to some of the details of this industry,—the fishermen gave them, as they unrolled their nets from the reels, or as we sat on the shingle beside them at the camp-fire. The cost of an outfit is, boat with sails and other gear, $225, three gangs of 12 nets at $300, $900, in all $1125. This is a very complete outfit and should, when worked by two

_____

(a) Henry's Travels and Adventures in Canada, 1760 to 1776, Vol. 1, 54.

7

or three men, take, in the season, 18 or 20 tons, worth
at the stations $70 to $80 a ton. The net is of four and
a-half inch mesh, according to law, is five feet broad,
weighted with lead, and has oiled, wooden floats. The
mesh is made in Kilbirnie, Scotland, and is worth $2.60
a pound. It is hung on No. 82 cotton cord. It takes
five hanks of cotton to hang one 7½ lb. net. This
would make the length of the gill net 1560 feet, or
the small gang of six nets would reach 9360 feet.
Each proprietor has his own color of buoy, one of
which, with a little flag attached, is placed at each
end of the gang and anchored. The nets are left out
two or three nights, or more if the sea be rough.
The fish caught are white fish, lake trout, pickerel,
catfish, herring, bass, and an occasional sturgeon.

The fishermen pay no rent or taxes and are under
regulations of the Dominion as to the time and mode
of fishing. They pay an annual license fee. November is the close season, and this is objected to because
the Americans have not the same close season and so
get the benefit of our law, as the fish know no boundary line. The large whitefish, of from 8 to 10 pounds
in weight, come into the shoals in November.

At some of the fish stations the entrails are boiled
down and fish oil made. At Squaw Island between
40 and 60 barrels, at the Bustards half that number,
or, on the average, one barrel to each vessel is made
annually, worth in Toronto $10 to $12 a barrel. So
malodorous is the process, that it is always carried on
at a distance from the places of residence. At Squaw

Island we saw the oil factory across the Bay. On the Bustards the perfume carried about by an old man from the Lewis Islands, proclaimed him master of the vats. He told us in broken English of his cottage, garden and two cows in a pleasant lake-side village, where his good wife had charge in his absence. Nor had he forgotten Stornoway and the herring fishing in his younger days off the Butt of Lewis in his native Hebrides. His calling here had a wonderful interest for the simple-minded old man, and he insisted on our visiting his den. Sitting in an oily scow, he took the oars, and passing out among some islands, and into a little bay enclosed with high rocks, we came to a shanty, with an iron crane over the doorway, and empty barrels about it. Landing, he ushered us into the rude laboratory. Noisome messes stewed slowly in two iron vats, crude oil rising to the surface. The good man proudly exhibited his apparatus, crane, vats, barrels and stock on hand. He stirred up the simmering rich stuff, in which he seemed as interested and as unconscious of any unpleasantness, as a painter mixing colors on his palette. Alas ! our unaccustomed senses could not abide the terrible odors that arose. Waiting till his back was turned, we escaped and were soon breathing purer air on an adjacent mossy rock-top.

The largest salmon trout taken in recent years in the Bay were two caught in 1892, by Messrs. Brown and Farr while fishing with nets on Snake Island shoals. Their joint weight was 110 pounds, "and I think," writes Mr. Adam Brown, "that there was not a pound of difference between the two fish." Alexander Henry refers to trout taken by his men with lines through holes in the ice in Lake Huron, weighing sixty pounds and upwards. While the catch is generally but a moderate recompense for the outfit and labour and some are disappointed, there are occasions when fortune smiles, so that the nets break with the contained fish. One such instance occurred last July ; William Proulx, a fisherman from Sarnia, upon the river St. Clair, worked for some time in the channel near Killarney. He was about to return home disappointed, when he perceived a school of whitefish, and at once hauled a seine and caught a ton, he threw again and so worked for about fourteen days with three assistants, bringing to the agents of the Buffalo Fish Co., Messrs. J. & C. Noble, who verify this statement, in one trip 4800 lbs. in another 4770 lbs. and in all 18 tons, which realized $1350 or more. Messrs. Noble state that " There has been no other such catch of fish in recent years."

In the autumn, pickerel are worth more per pound than any other fish here taken, for the peculiar reason that they can be exported undressed and so keep longer than the others. The Jews therefore buy them as the Rabbinical law prohibits the use of any meat, except such as the Hebrew butcher has prepared.

An attempt is made, under an Act of the Dominion Parliament and inspectors appointed to visit the fishing grounds, to hinder the wholesale destruction of the finny tribe. Seines are prohibited in certain seasons, trap and pound nets at all times, yet we heard sufficient to make us fear that many tons of fish are unlawfully taken in bays and rivers, and on shoals, where if allowed to spawn, they would add many thousand fold to their kind, and even in deep waters, a person alert, and with local knowledge, could find many pound and trap or fyke nets and many mischievous trespassers. A change in the mode of surveillance was suggested, by one who knows the circumstances, namely, the appointment of resident inspectors—one in charge of each station of thirty or more vessels, smaller stations to be grouped; each tug used in fishing to be counted as three sailing vessels, and a well paid and reliable visiting Captain with steam-cutter, to be placed over all in the lake and bay to enforce the law. The fishermen regard with favor the restocking of the waters from the Government Pisciculture stations, but this cannot keep pace with the loss caused by the fouling of the rivers and bay by the lumbermen with saw-dust and lumber refuse. The present wholesale destruction goes on, with but short cessation in November, and greedy evasion of the law. The fisheries, and the forests and land game, are under different jurisdictions, the first are controlled by the Dominion, the others by the Province, otherwise one set of Inspectors could look after, if not all, probably the fish and game with profit to the country. (*a*)

(*a*) Proof of official activity has been amusingly given since the "White Squall" was returned by our skipper to her owners. The vessel and outfit were seized and tied up for alleged poaching.

The use of steam and American capital in our inland fisheries is every year increasing. It would be well if the same time could be agreed on as the close season for the American, as well as the Canadian fishing in these waters.

As to the value of these fisheries Mr. George Johnson, Statistician of the Department of Agriculture and Commerce, Ottawa, has kindly furnished the writer the following information of date August 29th, 1892.

" The fisheries of the Georgian Bay and Lake Huron for 1880 and 1885, show the following result :

	1880. lbs.	1885. lbs.
Whitefish..........	4,813,978	4,079,640
Trout..............	3,555,300	6,519,780
Herring...........	442,600	2,835,650
Sturgeon	209,000	1,041,300
All other kinds.....	2,881,195	7,275,600
Total pounds.......	11,902,075	21,751,970
Total value........	$406,461	$903,795
Persons employed...	1,047	1,967
Steam tugs employed	12	25
Value steam tugs employed........	$16,700	$95,100
Boats, number......	307	890
Boats, value........	$38,008	$80,346
Nets and seines,value	$125,177	$241,253

" The above includes both the American and Canadian catch."

· Referring to the Government returns as to the
fisheries for 1890, we find that, in the Georgian Bay
Division, there were then employed 15 tugs, valued
at $39,400 and 152 boats valued at $29,040. There
were 738,600 fathoms of gill nets valued at $116,205;
and 465 fathoms of seines worth $550. The total value
of the catch is stated to be $530,500. The whitefish
taken weighed 2,858,000 pounds. Next in value were
the trout, 2,444,000 pounds, then the pickerel 464,300
pounds, and the remainder of the catch was made up
of bass, sturgeon, herring, pike, maskinonge and
"coarse fish." In the Lake Huron Division for the
same year there were 10 tugs and 131 boats employed. The total catch was worth $223,752, of which
the whitefish and trout made up the largest proportions.

In the fisheries of the Province 3045 men are employed, 436 being in the Georgian Bay, 427 in Lake
Huron, and the Manitoulin section had 387. The Bay
had the greatest number of fathoms of gill nets in
use.

The overseers complain of gangs of fishermen from
the United States who carry on extensive illegal fishing with spears and fyke nets, "They are," one official
report states, "protected by fish dealers, who are mostly
agents for American firms. Some seizures were made
but it is hard to locate the nets and seize them with
this class of poachers."

The total annual value of the fisheries in the Georgian Bay Division for 1890, is officially stated as

above, out of a total in the province of $2,009,637. The Georgian Bay stands at the head of the list in whitefish and lake trout. The revenue derived by the Dominion Government from rents, license fees and fines, within the Province of Ontario, amounted in 1890 to $23,666, out of a total in the Dominion of $57,000.

Mr. D. W. Port, of Toronto, who deals largely in fish, estimates the catch in the Georgian Bay for 1892 at nine millions of pounds. Averaging the value at four cents a pound, which is less than the government valuation just quoted, the receipts of the Bay fishermen for 1892 would be $360,000. He states that about one-third of this is consumed in Canada; the other two-thirds are shipped to the United States and are taken in free of duty, as they are represented or assumed to have been taken with American outfits, boats and nets, although not one-tenth of the men employed are Americans. The catch on the Canadian side of Lake Huron was, in 1892, as he thought from information received, about equal to that in the Georgian Bay. The Dominion Government has notified the fishermen that after the season of 1893, they must use five inch mesh, and not more than 6000 yards of nets to each boat.

Mr. Port admits that it is very hard to enforce restrictive measures on our shores, when the Americans give their fishermen full liberty to use small mesh nets and have practically no close season. He concludes with the suggestion that a strong effort should be made to have the same regulations enforced on both sides of the lakes, and then our valuable fisheries would continue to be profitable. The causes of loss or depletion in the fish supply, are to some extent uncontrollable; such as the changes in the conditions of life incident to the opening of the country, the removal of the forests and the resulting variation in the rain-fall. It is to such causes that the disappearance of salmon, once abundant in Lake Ontario, is attributed.

Spawning and feeding grounds are largely injured by sawdust and by decayed fish and offal. The laws requiring the consumption of mill refuse are sufficiently explicit, but too often fail in the enforcement.

The fishing is sometimes impeded in the Bay and North Channel by a fossil coral, having the appearance of a petrified sponge, in which the nets get caught. It is also found in abundance on the shores of the Grand Manitoulin. This fossil is the *Favosites hemispherica.*

CHAPTER VII.

WILD ANIMALS; BIRDS; FRUIT; FORESTRY; EXTENT AND
VALUE OF THE TIMBER; RAILWAY DEVELOPMENT;
CANALS PROPOSED; THE HURONTARIO SHIP RAIL-
WAY:

THE *feræ naturæ,* which formerly abounded in this part of Ontario, have become less plentiful on the south shore, but the north and east sides of the Bay are still the paradise of hunters. The moose, Alce Americanus, is generally conceded to be identical with the Swedish elk. He never frequented the south shore from choice. A country well watered by small lakes and streams, with ridges and upheavals, such as are common in the Laurentian ranges of hills, is chosen by him, as from these he obtains good views of the surrounding region.

(114)

He is found by the prospector voyageur and hunter in Northern Ontario, from the south edge of the Laurentians to the Height of Land. During the heat of summer he stands at mid-day in water in some quiet cove, or inland lake, cooling his feet and enjoying immunity from the annoying flies. On such occasions he appears motionless, but with eye intent on every intruder. In October the bull moose is to be avoided, as that is his honeymoon, and he is ready to fight for his mate with all who adventure near. He is then dangerous to approach, even when isolated, and many explorers, when not armed, have had narrow escapes, owing to his morose temper during this period.

Later in the autumn, he herds with his fellows, all discords are forgotten, the bulls feeling bound in honor to defend the cows and calves. A "moose yard" is then a bonanza for the hunter, generally an Indian, or half-breed, who may lay in his winter supply of meat, to be used fresh as long as the frost lasts, or smoked for later use.

Moose-hunting tests the sportsman's utmost skill. The moose is fleeter and more crafty than the deer. He has been tamed when caught young, and used as the reindeer by Hudson Bay employees and half-breeds in the North-West. The bellow of the bull moose is loud as the lion's roar, and can be heard from two to three miles across the lakes.

The full-grown bull is the size of a large horse. He is fully five feet in height, and weighs from 1,000 to 1,200 pounds. He browses on the leaves and twigs, and he likes the lily roots growing at the bottom of ponds. With his long upper lip he reaches under water for them, his body often entirely disappearing for some minutes. His antlers are a striking feature. They are most fully developed after the fifth year, measuring five feet from root to tip. They are cast in December or January, but so rapid is the growth, that a complete new set is formed by the following August.

The skin sells at 40c. per pound, but is generally used in making mocassins. From eight to twelve pairs can be made from each hide, for the use of the household or to sell at a good price.

A few wapiti, or American elk, and an occasional caribou, are found in the region under discussion, but are rapidly becoming extinct. The wapiti is also as large as a horse, with magnificent horns, and has been called the " antlered monarch of the waste." Red deer are very plentiful about the north and east sides of the Georgian Bay. The great hunting ground for them is north of it, and following easterly by the rivers coursing through the Muskoka and Parry Sound Districts, and the stretch of country between the South Ontario settlements and the Ottawa River and its tributaries, to, and into, the Quebec Province.

In a part of this region east of Muskoka, there is as much water as land, and this attracts the deer, who may avoid the wolf by escaping on the run-ways to the innumerable lakes, and drive off the tormenting fly by wading in the shallows. Here, too, he roams

. over the broad plateaus of Archæan rocks, covered with sweet herbage and shrubs.

Hunters hide near the run-ways, leading from lake to lake, and shoot as he passes, or watch with canoe at the coves, and secure the game as it takes the water. For the protection of the larger game, which was becoming scarce, an act, passed in April, 1892, prohibits the hunting of moose, elk, reindeer, or caribou in Ontario, until after the first day of November 1895.

The season for deer-hunting is also limited to the first fifteen days of November. In Ontario, still hunting is much in vogue, which requires a noiseless tread and alertness of eye and ear. The Indians and professional hunters and trappers, take bear, lynx, wild-cat, sable or marten, mink, ermine, weasel, fox, otter, fisher, wolverine, skunk, raccoon, musk-rat, and an occasional wolf. Indians are exempt from game laws, and may hunt when and where they please. So, also, settlers in unorganized districts may capture game for their families' use at all seasons. *(a)*

BIRDS OF THE GEORGIAN BAY.—While it is not

(a) We learn from Champlain's narrative, (Book III. 151,) that the range of the buffalo extended farther east in his day than in later times, even perhaps into the Nipissing district. He had not himself seen any, but saw their skins used for clothing on the Upper Ottawa, by Indians who described the animals and the places where they were slain. The limit of the northern habitat of the buffalo is generally stated to be 60°, but it was sometimes found as far north as 63° or 64°. The Hon. J. C. Schultz, of Manitoba, states that no buffalo has been seen east of the Red River of the North since 1865. The range of the musk ox is much farther north, seldom south of latitude 67°, and so well within the Arctic Circle.

intended to attempt a full ornithological account, or .
even list, of the birds of this region, we cannot pass
without a glance at the most remarkable of them. The
attention of the casual passenger is first attracted by
the gulls, which fly in the wake of vessels, picking
up such food as may be thrown on the water. The
common white gull is the American herring gull
(Larus Argentatus). It is abundant on all the lakes.
Its young are grey in color. The largest gull is
the great black-back gull (Larus Marinus). It visits
Ontario generally in the winter and spring, going far
north to breed. Bonaparte's gull (Larus Philadelphiae)
is a small, but plentiful, species that comes from the
south in spring and breeds in Canada. The gull called
by the fishermen the " garnet," is the common tern
(Sterna Hirundo); it has bright red bill and feet—
Bonaparte's gull also has some red on the feet. Fishermen gather gulls' eggs in large quantities in early
summer, and find them palatable so long as there are
not more than two eggs in a nest, after which they
are rancid.

There are three large owls which are more plentiful
in the Georgian Bay District than farther south,—
the great grey owl (Ulula Cinerea), the great horned
owl (Bubo Virginianus), and the snowy owl (Nyctea
Nivea, or Surnia). The commonest small owls are
the short-eared owl (Surnia Brachyotos), the hawk
owl (Asio Accipitrinus), the screech owl (Megascops .
Asio), and Richardson's owl (Nyctea Richardsoni).

The American hawk owl (Surnia Ulula), which is

very hawk-like in appearance, is plentiful in Muskoka and the Georgian Bay, though quite rare about Toronto. There is no auk usually found there, as this bird confines itself to the sea coast, only an occasional straggler visiting the lakes. We have, in the museum of the Canadian Institute, a specimen of the razor-billed auk (Alco Torda), which was taken about three years ago at Toronto.

There are two woodpeckers found around the Georgian Bay, that are rarely seen in South Ontario ; the artic three-toed [Picoides Arcticus] and the Pileated [Ceophlocus Pileatus]. The former, as its name implies, is a strictly Northern species ; the other, our largest wood-pecker, used to inhabit the whole province, but with the destruction of the forests, has retreated to the Northern part. The French call him *coq des bois*, cock of the woods.

The Canada jay or " Whiskey Jack " is common in Northern Ontario, though not found in the South, and in winter, frequents the lumber camps to pick up anything it can find in the way of food.

Many of the finches and warblers, that pass north in the spring, breed in the Georgian Bay District, and call on us again in the fall on their way to the South. The pine grosbeak is a regular visitor there, though it only comes south to Lake Ontario once in five or six years. These birds were plentiful in Toronto in the winter of 1889 and 1890. The more beautiful evening grosbeak (*Coccothraustes Vespertina*), also then visited Southern Ontario, but has not been seen here in any numbers since. This bird will dwell contentedly in captivity, but its habitat being strictly northern, it droops as the warm weather comes on, and seldom lasts in its cage through the summer.

The loon or great northern diver, is common on all these waters, but Lake Nipissing is its favorite resort. Its plaintive note is known to all. So quick are its movements that it generally escapes the rifle ball by diving. Thirty years ago and more, wild pigeons selected the shores of the Bay as their breeding ground. Early settlers remember large areas of virgin forests appropriated for the purpose. The noise and odor were perceived a mile off. Twenty nests were often on one tree, three or four on a single bough. The people of Toronto frequently witnessed in the spring, clouds upon clouds of pigeons coming northwards across Lake Ontario. Flocks a mile in length by a hundred yards in breadth, were seen passing over. Many rested in the suburban woods, after their long flight of nearly forty miles across the lake, and a hundred miles or more beyond, going to the northern breeding grounds. Their course has been changed to a route west of Lake Superior in consequence of the grain wave developing west-ward. The naturalists, Wilson and Audubon, describe masses of pigeons, migrating in countless swarms, eclipsing the sun, breaking trees as they alighted amid the shouts of people, the screeches of hawks and eagles and the howls of wild beasts. Wilson estimated one flock to contain some millions of birds. Their flight

was at the rate of fully sixty miles an hour. The
young were fed in their nests with seed grain lately
planted, carried by the parents, who went, one at a
time, to distances of five to ten miles to get it. The
farmers found them very troublesome, and had often
to plant their grain crops twice.

Before grain was grown, on what did they feed it
may be asked ! The pigeon berry, omni-present on
the Laurentian, as well as on the Huronian formation,
indeed from the great lakes to Labrador, was their main
reliance. This plant grows in areas miles in extent,
and is often in close clusters. The berry, when ripe,
is scarlet and the size of a pea. When a handful
is eaten, a pleasing pine-apple flavour is perceived.
The flower has a slight perfume when in its first
bloom. It retains, in most soils, its delicate appearance for two months. The pigeons also fed on cranberries and red ash berries, and on the dark purple
seed of nana fruit, or shad berry, found in marshes.
The shad berry may be classed with the medlars, and is
like the lilac in size of its bush, leaf, and habit ; the
bloom in spring is a creamy white and very fragrant,
not dissimilar to the elder-berry in appearance. The
fruit is heart-shaped of the size of a water-melon
seed, and held in large clusters. It is a variety of the
Amelanchier Canadensis.

The " honk " of wild geese is heard over the Bay
in the early spring and autumn, but their breeding
ground is farther north. They feed on the wild
vetch bean and vine of James Bay, and of the Hudson Bay and its tributary waters and islands.

8

The Anserinæ of Ontario are divided into the Canada goose, or Bernicula Canadensis ; Hutchin's goose, the brant, the snow-goose, blue-winged-goose and American white-fronted goose. They come north in March and April, returning in November. During the journey they stop at feeding grounds for a week or two at a time, and it is then they may be seen on the Georgian Bay, and its tributary waters. Within fifty years past they were well known in the Toronto Bay.

Mrs. Jameson relates, in the story of her Canadian residence referred to, that as she sat at her window overlooking the water on the 19th, May, 1837, she saw flights of wild geese passing over, and great black loons, skimming diving, and sporting, on the bosom of the Bay.

These birds seem to have then spent some time on the lower waters, as they generally came with the breaking up of the ice and remained until the summer set in. In the season referred to Mrs. Jameson states that the ice had been broken and swept out of Toronto harbour, and the first steam vessel of the year had entered it, on the fifteenth of the previous April.

Swans fly over Ontario, to their breeding grounds in the north, but generally pass further west than the Bay, and are very seldom taken in its waters. They are of two varieties, the whistler swan [Olor Columbianus] and the trumpeter swan [Olor Buccinator.]

The duck family is very largely represented in

Northern Ontario. They come from the rice fields of Georgia and Mississippi, from the marshes of Maryland, from the Pacific Coast, the Isthmus of Panama, Guatemala, Cuba and the West Indies. Among them are the mallard, the black duck, the gadwell or grey duck, the widgeon, the spoonbill, the blue-winged and green-winged teal, the wood duck, the canvas back, the American golden-eye, and the longed-tailed duck or old squaw.

The grouse, called partridge in Canada, is common in Ontario. The ruffed grouse is that generally met with. Its habitat is the forests and swamps, from the United States to the Arctic Sea. It is generally in flocks of eight to ten. When disturbed they fly into trees. In summer the food of this bird is berries of various kinds, in the winter the buds of spruce and fir. The spruce partridge, a smaller and darker bird, has the same range, but is less common. Plover and snipe gather on the shores of the Bay, in the autumn, and remain some weeks before migrating to the South. Large black ravens, often quite tame, are about the lumber camps, and are made pets of by the hardy axe-men. Humming-birds of an exquisite plumage hover over the flowers in sunny nooks. The melancholy cry of the whippoorwill came through the woods each night. Rabbits, so called, are numerous in many places. They are grey, changing to white in winter. The species met are the Lepus Sylvaticus, wood-hare or cotton-tail, and the Lepus Americanus, or American hare. The pine-squirrel and ground-squirrel, or chipmunk are the smallest of their kind north of the Bay, and take the places of the large red and black varieties found south of Collingwood. The flying squirrel, and grey squirrel are seldom seen in this region.

FLOWERS, FRUIT AND FORESTRY.—The flowers and wild fruit met with have been referred to in the previous narrative. Were we to describe the mosses of Northern Ontario, a volume would be needed, there being hundreds of varieties of moss on trees and rocks and springs. Their little spires each stand out and shine as rosebuds, and the weary foot rests on the lovely bed softer than eider down. (a) But we cannot do more than glance at some of the more important plants here found. Next to the whortleberry, pronounced " huckle-berry," and the raspberry, the pigeon berry, already referred to, is probably the most valuable of the native fruits, its bright green carpeting large areas, and covering a succulent nourishing berry which is of great service to any one out of food and ammunition. The South shore of the Bay is among the best fruit regions in Canada ; its apples, pears, plums, cherries and grapes are of the best. The timber, which grows on the shores of the Bay, is mainly white and red or Norway pine, spruce, cedar, hemlock, tamarack, white and black birch, beech, maple and poplar. On the North Shore these maintain their size and vigour. The old forests, on the

---

(a) Note Virgil Ecl. VII. 45, Muscosi fontes, et somno mollior herba.

banks of the **Nottawasaga**, Beaver and Sydenham
rivers, were noted for their stately elms, oaks, hickories, beeches and maples, large in girth, tall and
straight in stem, till they soared above the silver-
skinned birches, iron-woods and other smaller trees.
Then the branches spread out their foliage, which
interlacing, largely excluded the summer rays from
the soil beneath, preserving moisture in the ground
until late in the spring, an essential condition of tree
life. Most of the forest trees are nourished at the
earth's surface, the thick layers of fallen leaves collecting one upon another, year after year, furnishing the
potash and other food absorbed by the ganglia of
roots spread out laterally beneath them. In the rich
compost below these trees, the delicate hepatica,
violet, trillium, wintergreen, and other wild flowers,
spring. The dark green of the may-flower or trailing
arbutus, also called ground-laurel, spreads a sweet-
scented carpet over the rocks. This creeping vine
was the first flower that attracted the Pilgrim Fathers
on their landing in New-England. They called it the
May Flower after the vessel which had brought
them to America. It inhabits rocky and sandy soil.
In sunny glades are the wild cherry, pinberry,
currant, plum, shadberry, gooseberry and strawberry.
As the standing timber is removed, the sun's glare
reaches the light leafy soil covering the clays, gravels
and marls, and the carbonates developed by nature's
alchemy. The north-east winds get full play, and
the remaining trees also cease to flourish, and in time,

make way for a new growth of poplars and evergreens. Sugar maples which have reached fully 200
years, are found in the primeval forests, oaks and
elms of twice that age, and pines and spruce older yet
as shewn by the rings of annual growth. Some of the
green monsters still standing had celebrated their first
centennial, when Columbus crossed the Atlantic,
and may have sheltered Champlain and his Huron
hordes, as they passed this way.(a) When the older
timber is removed, the tulip tree and English elm
may be introduced, along the southern margin of
the Bay, as they have been on both sides of Lake
Ontario. Forty-five years ago, during a remarkably
warm and dry summer, an extensive fire began in the
Lake Superior country, and advancing easterly, ran
along the north shore continuously during the entire
season. It swept over an area of five hundred miles
in length and one hundred in width. The smoke
materially interfered with navigation on the lakes
and Bay. Animal, as well as vegetable life, was
destroyed, the soil itself being in many places burned
down to the rock. Traces of the ravages so wrought

(a) "The red pine near Barrie, and through all the Penetanguishene country, grows to an enormous size. I measured one near
Barrie no less than 26 feet in girth, and its height at least 200 feet,
and this was merely a chance one by the path-side."—Sir R. Bonny-
castle—*Canada and the Canadians in 1846.*

Mr. Linton counted the rings of an oak felled midway between
Lake Ontario and the Georgian Bay. He calculated that it had
been a sapling about the time when Sir William Wallace and Robert
Bruce were defending their native land.—*Life of a Backwoodsman.*

The white spruce attains an age exceeding 400 years in the Arctic
altitudes before it shews signs of decay.—Sir J. Richardson, Arctic
Expedition, Vol. II. 316.

are visible still on the north shore. The fire was only arrested in the low lands by the Autumn rains. Entire forests of dead pines upon elevated ridges still stand with blackened trunks and attest the whole-sale devestation. During the construction of the line of the Canadian Pacific Railroad along the north shore, forest fires were frequent and very destructive.

Meliboeus happily addressed his friend as he reclined under the spreading beech :

" Tityre, tu, patulæ recubans sub-tegmine fagi." (*a*)

nor have we any shade more refreshing in the dog-days than that of the beech, with its outstretched horizontal boughs, and green mat of leaves, palpitat-ing in the August air. Probably the most beautiful tree in our forest is the

" Vast Elm, impervious to daylight's beams,
Where live the Visions, and where haunt the Dreams." (*b*)

The Elm's festooning boughs hang down over the waters of the small lakes and streams fifty to sixty feet, the leaves in Indian summer being of mellow yellow in strong contrast with the vines, which cling to their trunks, and whose foliage is scarlet.

The white oak, rising without a lateral branch for fifty feet, and spreading out as far above with bushy dark green head rustling in the breeze, is the synonym of majestic strength.

(*a*) Virgil ; Eclogue 1.

(*b*) Virgil ; translated by W. B. Phipps in Report on Replant-ing Forests, 1883, p. 11.

Charles G. D. Roberts, sings the praises of the maple, one of the embles of the Canadian flag.

> " Oh tenderly deepen the woodland glooms
> And merrily sway the beeches ;
> Breathe delicately the willow blooms,
> And the pines rehearse new speeches,
> The elms toss high, till they brush the sky,
> Pale catkins the yellow birch launches,
> But the tree I love, all the greenwood above
> Is the maple of sunny branches.
>
> The maple, it glows, with the tint of the rose,
> When pale are the spring-time regions,
> And its towers of flame from afar proclaim,
> The advance of winter's legions."

When in the open, as at Tamarac Cove, shrubs and many colored flowers were on all sides. Birds flew from twig to twig, butterflies and bees hovered over their dewy cups. Passing a little from the shore, all was still, save the occasional chatter of a squirrel, or the tapping of the red-headed wood-pecker in the great ever-green groves about us. Miss Johnston, our Mohawk poetess, expresses the feeling engendered by the occasion—

> " The littleness of language seems the flower ;
> The firs are silence, grandeur, soul and power."

Upon the islands, and the edges of smaller lakes, near the north shore, the lesser vegetation puts on, in early autumn, a very varied dress of scarlet, rich yellow, dark red, and brown. The greens of the pine and spruce in the back ground, intermingle with the brighter colors and frame a picture exhibiting nature's most artistic skill. These lakelets seem then, as the western sun shines on them, like emeralds set among other richest gems. A river which crosses the Canadian Pacific, twenty miles west of Sudbury, and passes into Vermilion Lake, one of the reservoirs of the north branch of the Spanish River, is named Vermilion from the color of its creeping vines.

In Mrs. Jameson's description of her excursion through the Bay in 1837, in the canoe of Mr. Jarvis, Indian Superintendent, she expresses frequent delight at the exhibition of beauty among the rocks; " In the clefts and hollows grew quantities of gooseberries and raspberries, wild roses, the crimson columbine, a large species of harebell, a sort of willow, juniper, birch and stunted pine; and such was the usual vegetation." (Vol. 3, 326.) This traveller's experience related only to the productions of the rocky shores and islands and not to the interior.

The timber interest is now more important in this region than the fishing industry. Ontario gets for this valuable product a large annual income. It is, indeed, a main source of revenue of the Province. Many lumbermen have done well in the business; some of them have become millionaires. The wholesale cutting and deportation goes on apace, and necessarily so under present conditions, as the encroachment of settlements renders bush fires more common. The surveyors often find that a considerable portion of the timber has been scorched and more or less injured.   In the township of Porter, surveyed in 1891, one thousand acres are reported as *brule*, and the proportion is often larger than in this case.

The employment of fire Rangers, about one hundred in number, at joint expense of the Province and timber licensees, has proved beneficial.   These officers go through the great woods and use every means to protect them against the ravages of fire.   When timber is scorched, but still standing, they can secure most of its value, by having it made into logs and taken to market before the busy " borer" insect commits its ravages, and decay ensues.   The Rangers are also of service in guarding the forests from poaching lumbermen, who, in old times, removed millions of feet of lumber without license or payment of any fee.   The fact that only a very limited supply of timber remains in the formerly great pineries of Michigan and Wisconsin, and that much American capital now seeks investment in our northern limits, makes their preservation and proper use yearly more and more a matter of capital importance.

The timber on the public lands may be placed on the market as soon as the lands are surveyed.   It is usual to sell by auction, after public notice, the right to cut and remove the timber within a township or other considerable space, called a timber limit or berth. In addition to the sum paid at the time of purchase, the buyer pays an annual ground rent of $3 per square mile, so long as he works the limit, and $1.25 for each thousand feet, board measure, for the timber taken. In October, 1892, the Government sold two limits, the township of Morgan, of 35¼ square miles, which realized $373,650, and the township of Lumsden, 31¼ square miles, for which the sum of $96,875 was received. These limits are about fifty miles north of the Georgian Bay. The difference in price realized is attributable to the quantity and quality of the timber, which depends largely on the nature of the soil. Lumsden being more rocky and sterile than the better wooded Morgan limit. The total collections of the Government for 1891 in the Woods and Forests branch throughout Ontario, amounted to $1,022,619, which sum includes $172,551 for bonuses, showing the revenue for timber dues, rent, etc., to be $850,068. (a)

In 1892 the pine on other limited areas north of the Bay was sold, together with timber in other districts, the Provincial Treasury so realizing a sum exceeding $2,250,000 by way of bonuses, the prices paid being high beyond precedent.

The great lumber region of Ontario extends to the north of Lake Abbitibbe and westward fully seven hundred miles to the Lake of the Woods and Rainy River country. The town of Rat Portage is at its western extremity and possesses unrivalled water power for saw-mills and grist-mills. It is on the line of the Canadian Pacific Railway between Lake Superior and Winnipeg.

The white pine region again extends eastward as

(a) Report of Hon. A. S. Hardy, Commissioner of Crown Lands, Ont., 1891, VI.

far as the head waters of the **Madawaska** and **Ronne-
chere**, which rivers largely drain the country east of
the **Pettawawa**, which is a tributary of the Ottawa
river.   Thus the base line of the timber region of the
Province is about one thousand miles in length.

If a line were drawn from the mouth of the Severn,
on the East side of the Georgian Bay, due north,
such line would pass by North Bay, the chief Town
on Lake Nipissing.   It would thence go through Lake
Temiscamingue; over the Height of Land and through
Lake Abbitibbe to the south margin of James Bay.
The country on either side of this line to North Bay
is wholly Laurentian, containing many lakes and
streams upon the sides of which there is a considerable
quantity of agricultural land, moderately settled.
Much timber is annually taken from this region.

Many towns and villages have sprung up, sustained
by the lumbering interest.   These are mostly along
the course of the Northern and Pacific Junction Railway which joins the main road near North Bay.
This Town is so called from the Bay of that name on
Lake Nipissing, and numbers 2500 inhabitants.

The Nipissing is a somewhat shallow sheet of water
containing white-fish and salmon trout   Upon its
shores is some excellent land.   Its waters escape
through the picturesque Nipissing, or French River
into the Georgian Bay.   They flow over a mass of
islands and ridges of rocks which sometimes span the
entire width of the stream.   This lake and the
various channels of French River were surveyed

by the late Alexander Murray, F.G.S. and he gave the names they bear to many places in the country north of Lake Huron, which he was the first to lay down correctly on the map. Of the rivers flowing into Lake Nipissing, the Sturgeon has a length of about one hundred miles and is much used in moving timber. A creek, at the north-east end of the lake, together with the three small lakes, called Trout, Turtle and Talons, and the Mattawan River, which connects them with the Ottawa River, have had an historic past. For many centuries the Algonquins and their predecessors passed by this route in their birch canoes, to attack rival tribes on the debatable ground to the south of the Georgian Bay.

On the ninth of July, 1615, Samuel de Champlain embarked at the isle of Ste. Helene, opposite Hochelaga, passed with his party up the Ottawa, entered the Mattawan and through it and the water course mentioned, reached Lake Nipissing. Thence he coursed along the Easterly shore of the Georgian Bay to the Huron Territory. Here he joined the warriors in hunting, and in their memorable expedition against the Iroquois in the State of New York. Sir George Simpson, Governor of the Hudson Bay Company, took the same route to the mouth of French River, and then along the North Shore and Channel to Sault Ste. Marie and the western posts. North Bay was an important Hudson Bay Station. The creek referred to is called *Riviere de Vase.* It is a muddy stream, and may be found four miles east of the Town of North Bay, where the Northern and Pacific Junction road joins the main line of the Canadian Pacific Railway. The route referred to was part of the northerly main line of communication between the waters of the Atlantic and the Pacific coast. It was through a game country where meat and fish were in great abundance. In July and August the whortle, or blue-berry, could be gathered in handfuls from bushes knee-high, on all the ridges and rocks. Raspberries and other wild fruit came to maturity in August, and these were a fair substitute for a more complete vegetable diet. The Mattawan route has many portages, and in returning from the west by this river, the trading canoes were unladen and borne around the obstructions on the shoulders of the crew, usually composed of seven men.

Some articles were carried in the canoe, and some in the hands of the voyageurs, but the heavy packs of skins, proceeds of the winter's hunt, were left at the beginning of the portage, necessitating a return of the men for that purpose.

On the return trip, the fur packs were exchanged for bales of cloth, of scarlet, red, blue and black, and other goods used in trading for peltries.

The long frail crafts could, with skilful management, withstand the heavy seas of the large lakes, which they had often to encounter, as in many places no landing could be made for several miles owing to the rocky character of the coast. These canoes were confined to the great lakes and rivers. At the head of

Lake Superior bulk was broken, and the packages destined for Red River and the Saskatchewan were transferred to smaller canoes. (*a*) The canoes sailed in brigades for mutual protection, six to ten in a fleet, whose crews might, as occasion arose, aid each other, and in case of mishap to any vessel, transfer its cargo and distribute the packages amongst the other canoes.

As the brigades approach their destination, having successfully made the St. Lawrence, and are lazily dropping down on its broad bosom to La Prairie, the fur-entrepôt of Montreal, gaudy shirts of blue or red, worsted sashes, placed double round the waist, new deer-skin gaiters, spotless white tanned mocassins and a gay *tuke* or *bonnet rouge*, are donned by the light-hearted voyageur. What now of the mothers, sisters and other dear ones, who, as the home-coming is announced in advance, hasten to meet and to greet him who, for two long years, has been absent and perhaps unheard of ? Has he gone with the Sieur de Champlain to fight the Mohawk in the Oneida country ? Has death claimed him as he too hardily attempted to shoot the Winnipeg or Mattawan, or braved the waves of Lake Superior ? Or, has his heart been left with a dusky maiden of the friendly Huron nation ? How many thousands of Indians have, in old days,

---

(*a*) Twelve hundred men, says McKenzie, were sometimes assembled at the Grand Portage, often indulging in the free use of liquor, and quarrelling with each other, yet always respecting their employers, who were comparatively few in number. Here the "Northmen" or "Winterers" with their furs met the "Pork-Eaters" or "Goers and Comers," as those were named who performed the journey between the Grand Portage and Montreal.

traversed the great route between the St. Lawrence
and Lake Huron in war-paint and feathers, or later,
as voyageurs aiding their half-brothers, the *bois-
brules*, in propelling their light barks, or in carrying
their packs over portages ! Their ancient course near
the Nipissing is as well marked on the rocks worn by
the travel of innumerable feet, though always clad in
soft mocassins, as if made but a year ago.

Nor has the advancing spirit of modern commerce
found any better route, for the steam-engine seeks to
follow, as nearly as possible, the same course. Over
it are now borne the wheat and cattle of the prairies,
the wares of European make, and the goods of China
and Japan. The various railways connecting Georgian Bay points now constructed, or in contemplation,
are subsidiary to the great central line largely con-
trolling the trade current of the upper half of the
North American continent. The fact that along our
north-shore and by the old voyageur route, was and
is the true and natural course of commercial exchange
and travel from continent to continent, was boldly
stated not long since by a Canadian railway magnate
of marked ability and foresight, in the city of Boston.
His assertion was not contradicted, and could not be
disproved. The opening of a route for vessels through
French River, Lake Nipissing and the rivers Mattawan
and Ottawa by the construction of the necessary canals, was advocated at one time, but the plan proved
impracticable owing to the vast amount of granite in
the way.

Then a Toronto and Georgian Bay Ship Canal was

proposed as a means for passing grain-laden vessels from the west to Lake Ontario, but the great cost involved in this work was fatal to its construction.

A third plan is now before the public, the Hurontario Ship Railway from Nottawasaga Bay to the mouth of the Humber . River, on the western boundary of Toronto. On this, when constructed, large vessels, with their cargo, crew and passengers, are to be placed and transferred from the Bay to the waters of Lake Ontario.

The late Captain J. B. Eads prepared a topographical model of the proposed railway which was publicly exhibited. It has been pronounced entirely feasible by eminent engineers, among whom are Messrs. J. W. Babcock and E. L. Corthell of Chicago, and Mr. Kivas Tully, C. E., of Toronto.

Referring to this project the *London Times* said : " We have said this scheme is a bold one, but it is not more remarkable for its boldness, as well as for its originality, than for its engineering soundness. . . . . A careful inspection of the details of this great work will convince the most sceptical that the project is both possible and practicable." The distance between the mouth of the Humber and the entrance to the Nottawasaga River is 66 miles, and the route surveyed was declared by Captain Eads to be remarkably favorable for such an undertaking. Practical consideration of this interesting project awaits the result of the completion of the Chignecto Ship Railway now in course of construction in Nova Scotia, from Bay Verte, on Northumberland Strait, to the Bay of Fundy.

9

CHAPTER VIII.

THERE is an incident of peculiar historical interest connected with the old Ottawa route. The renowned Champlain made his first trip up that river as far as the present site of Pembroke, about two years before the journey already referred to. He left Ste. Helen's Island on the 27th of May, 1613, with a party of four Frenchmen and one Indian.

Before proceeding far he exchanged one of the Frenchmen for an Indian, who left a war party to join him.

(138)

CHAMPLAIN'S ASTROLABE

(HALF DIAMETER OF ORIGINAL)
LOST JUNE 1613   FOUND AUGUST 1867
ON THE PORTAGE FROM THE OTTAWA RIVER TO
MUSKRAT LAKE.

At various stages in his course he took observations
for latitude, which are noted in his journal. At
Lachine he records the latitude observed as 45 degrees
18 minutes, which is only 5 minutes less than the
true latitude of that place. Arrived at the Chaudiere,
he describes the great waterfall in all its grandeur.
It was not then encroached upon by bridges, saw-
mills and acres of lumber-piles, as is at present the
case. At what is now the busy town of Hull, across
the river from the City of Ottawa, in full view of the
Parliament Buildings of the Dominion, but then a
primeval forest, he notes an observation which differs
from the true latitude by about 12 minutes. The
errors stated are insignificant, when the imperfection
of the instruments then in use is considered.

On the 6th of June, Champlain and his party passed
the island called by him St. Croix, where the river
was a league and a half broad, made some portages,
and paddled by a number of other islands of various
sizes. " Here," he writes, " our savages left the sacks
containing their provisions and their less necessary
articles, in order to be lighter for going over land."
They had proceeded along the west side of the Ottawa,
up the Cheneux Rapids to Goold's Landing, about
two miles below Portage du Fort. Here they dis-
embarked to take the route by the Muskrat Portage and Lake, to avoid the rapids and falls in the main
river. The course from this was very irksome, owing
to the many portages necessary, and to a windfall of
uprooted trees in the way. Four small lakes were

passed, when the party rested for a night, and then
proceeded through Muskrat Lake, where they were
entertained by Nibachis, an Indian chief, and in-
spected the rude dwellings made of the bark of trees,
and the cultivated fields of his people, where Champlain found Indian-corn, squashes, beans and peas
growing.

He then visited Tessouat, the great Algonquin
chief, and his settlement, with its graveyard and gar-
dens, on Allumette Island, in the Ottawa. Here he
disclosed to the warriors the main object of his trip,
namely, to obtain guides and a convoy to enable him
to reach the "North Sea." It was only three years
previous that Henry Hudson, the intrepid navigator,
steering westward from Greenland, had entered the
great bay, since bearing his name. Here his crew
mutinied, placed Hudson, with his son and some others
who adhered to him, in a small boat and left them to
the mercy of the waves and savages. No trace of the
unfortunate party was afterwards discovered.

Champlain hoped to reach the sea from the south.
Properly supported he might have done so, and raised
the French flag on the shores of James Bay, but to
his mortification, the Indians, through fear of northern
tribes, which feeling he could not overcome, refused
to venture with him. Champlain, therefore, soon retraced his steps back to the St. Lawrence.

At Goold's Landing, Champlain took an observation
which is the last noted on this voyage, and which is
erroneous by more than a degree of latitude. The

reason for this seems to be that during the difficulties
of the toilsome march he had lost his astrolabe. It
was dropped on a portage, or left with other articles
in a cache, in order to lighten the burdens (a). Here
it lay, protected in the wilderness by a pine tree
which grew up over the spot, for 254 years. Then
the tree fell, its stump decayed, and a farmer plowing
past it, disturbed the relics hidden for two centuries
and a half. The astrolabe was found in 1867 on lot
number twelve in the second range of the Township
of Ross, in the County of Renfrew, about two miles
southerly from Muskrat Lake. The railway station,
called Cobden, is within a league of the place. Mr.
R. S. Cassels, now of Toronto, secured the astrolabe
from the man who had found it, and he has it still.
The farmer's children had used the figured disk as a
plaything, and neighbors had puzzled over it and
pronounced it a strange surveyor's tool. For a time
Mr. Cassels was doubtful of its use and ignorant of its
history. Then his ingenious and learned friend, the
late Mr. A. J. Russell, saw and made a study of it.
His interest was aroused ; he discussed the matter
with instrument makers and with some French
savants of Montreal. He next went to Quebec, and
in the Laval library, as Mr. Cassels understood, read
the records of the travels of Champlain, and thus
learned the story of the loss of the astrolabe.

It is of plate brass, dark with age, in diameter

(a) *Voyages of Samuel de Champlain*, translated by C. P. Otis, III.
63 to 74 : *Champlain's Astrolabe*, by A. J. Russell, Montreal, 1879.

nearly six inches. The date, 1603, is engraved on it.
It is fully described by the translator and editor, Mr.
Otis, in the " voyages " referred to, as also in three
learned brochures, one by Rev. Dr. Scadding, one by
Mr. O. H. Marshall, and the third by Mr. Russell.
Utensils of thin copper, much oxydized, found with
the astrolabe, had been used in repairing the bottom
of a canoe. Some silver cups, with an engraving on
them, probably a crest, were sold for a trifle to a Brock-
ville pedlar, who, not dreaming of their value, melted
them for the metal.

The first application of the Astrolabe by Europeans
to navigation was made, according to Washington
Irving, in 1481. Seamen could by its use ascertain
the distance of the sun from the equator. Four years
later, Columbus used it, and advanced into unknown
seas with confidence, being able to trace his course by
means of the compass and astrolabe (*a*). This instrument has since been improved and modified into the
modern quadrant.

Mr. Cassels' interesting relic is no doubt the only
specimen of the kind in America. A similar astrolabe
was, it is reported, found in Valentia harbour, Ireland, and is supposed to have belonged to a ship of
the Spanish Armada. A short treatise on the astrolabe and its use, may be found in the works of
Geoffrey Chaucer. It is addressed to his son Louis, a
bright boy of ten years. (*b*)   But this instrument is

(*a*) Irving's Life of Columbus, VI. 63.
(*b*) Chaucer's treatise on the astrolabe is in the old English of

of more ancient origin than any date quoted. Dr. W. Smith, late archæologist of the British Museum, relates in his published works that he discovered in the palace of Sennacharib, excavated under a village on the hill of Kouyungic, among other treasures of antiquity, part of an astrolabe. Its circumference was divided into twelve parts, corresponding with the signs of the zodiac, the degrees of each being marked, and with an inner circle naming prominent stars. (*a*) It is now evident, as Mr. Russell remarks in the pamphlet referred to, that astronomical science and lore were not original with the Assyrians, but inherited by that conquering race from a more ancient people whose literature and arts of civilization they adopted, as Europeans have since cherished the learning of Greece and Rome.

Mr. Russell further remarks : " The astrolabe was found in general use among the Southern Arabians, by Vagues di Gama, when he discovered the way round the Cape of Good Hope to India, known in the

---

the year 1391, and begins thus : " Little Louis, my son, I perceive by certain evidences, thine ability to learn sciences touching numbers and proportions, and have considered thy busy prayer in special to learn the use of the astrolabie.".... " I am but a poor compilator of the labours of old astronomers, and have translated into English only for thy instruction, and with this sword shall I slay envy." As to the mode of holding the instrument, in taking the altitude of the sun, Chaucer says : " Put the ring of thine astrolabie upon thy right thumb, and turn thy left side against the light of the sun."

(*a*) The present director of the Assyrian branch of the British Museum does not share with the late Dr. Smith this opinion, but informed Mr Arthur Harvey, of Toronto, during a recent visit to the museum, that the Assyrian relic referred to was now generally regarded as a magical instrument only.

days of Pharaoh Necho."... "While we look upon this astrolabe as a relic of the founder of civilized society in Canada, her greatest man and most daring explorer, and while we regard it with additional interest as a memento of early adventure on what was, even then, Canada's great interior highway of commerce, and is, by the same destiny now, the site of our great Pacific Railway, we may also look upon it as a relic of ancient and even prehistoric science and civilization."

Proceeding north from North Bay we have for our guidance the observations made by an eminent engineer, Mr. J. C. Bailey, C. E., who surveyed this region at the instance of the Nipissing and James Bay Railway Company early in 1889. He has kindly placed his memoranda of the trip at our disposal, saying: "It is a beautiful land full of possibilities in mineral, agricultural, and other wealth. And yet, with a heritage so rich, with its forests of pine and valuable hard-wood, its buried treasures of minerals known to exist, its millions of acres of the very finest land, why this should be allowed to remain so long in its primeval state is a mystery to me. It is almost within "rifle-shot" of civilization, still there are no means to develop this valuable territory. The building of the railway will open up this almost impenetrable region, will furnish timber in exhaustless quantities, maintain a numerous and hardy population, and add millions of productive acres to the assessment rolls of the province!" The distance from North Bay to Moose Factory on James Bay is 350 miles. Moose Harbour will be about the same distance from Toronto as that city is from Quebec.

The products of the whale and other fisheries of Hudson Bay, as also of the mines and forests on the islands and shores of James Bay, and of the excellent dairy country between the Height of Land and James Bay will, by this road, be brought to the markets of Canada and the United States. Mr. Bailey's trip was preferably made in the winter, as he has found that the best season for such surveys. Lakes and rivers can then be crossed with facility on the ice, the trees are free from foliage, which would obstruct the view, and there are then no flies to annoy. Snow shoes were used and toboggans, on which the packs of provisions, clothing, and other necessaries, were put and drawn. The following is an extract from this remarkable account :

" At our very start from North Bay we found good land, and it continued so in large quantities to the end of our journey. We were still more surprised to find much valuable timber—belt after belt of red and white pine, groves of tamarac and spruce, with black and yellow birch, together with black and white ash, maple and whitewood. The tamarac and spruce were the largest and finest trees I have ever seen, and would be very valuable manufactured into lumber. Railway ties of tamarac can be counted by millions. . . . There are innumerable water powers, which will no doubt, as the material is here, be utilized in various manufactures, such as pulp mills, saw mills, quarrying and dressing stone and slate. The country can boast, too, of magnificient scenery. Then with its endless chain of lakes—deep, pure and cool water—its fishing, shooting, and healthy climate, it must become one of the most attractive resorts for sportsmen, pleasure-seekers, invalids, and those immediately connected with the opening up of the mines, and when once made accessible by the railway, it cannot fail to attract tourists and others from all parts of the Dominion as well as the United States. . . .

"It is almost impossible to give any idea as to the number, extent and beautiful scenery of these lakes, all of which teem with fish. Lake Tamagamingue has been used for fifty years or more by the Hudson Bay Company, in supplying fish to the other posts. This and Rabbit Lake are full of the finest species of whitefish and salmon trout, and the small streams running into these lakes, as I was informed by the Indians, are full of speckled trout. As to the game, I can say a little about this myself. There are moose there by thousands, also caribou and red deer. Fur-bearing animals, such as beavers, otters, minks, martens, foxes, wolves and wildcats are there in large numbers. We frequently met with little animals caught in the traps set by the Indians, taken them out, hung them up on trees and reset the traps; some of them were beautiful specimens of martens. Beavers were very plentiful there still."

Westward from Lake Temiscamingue about sixteen miles is Lake Tamagamingue. Unlike the former lake, which is but an enlargment of the Ottawa river, Tamagamingue is a large sheet of water with extensive bays and many islands, some of them considerable in size, and many of them mineral-bearing. The waters of this lake branch out north and south about thirty miles, and more than half that distance east and west. The Montreal river drains the country north-west of the Ottawa between these lakes. There are immense tracts of agricultural lands on the margins of these lakes and rivers. The Blanche, which empties into Lake Temiscamingue, passes through a good agricultural country and is navigable for twenty-five miles. The clay lands in its valley are estimated to be from

500 to 600 square miles in area, or equal to twelve
townships, each of 32,000 acres. (*a*) The available
agricultural land on the Montreal River is equal in
extent to fifteen ordinary townships. Rabbit Lake
which is between the two large lakes just mentioned,
is in the midst of a great white pine region. The
country south of Temiscamingue was found by Mr.
Bailey to contain excellent land with timber of white
pine, black and yellow birch, spruce and tamarac in
large quantity. The temperature is dry, and the cold
is not felt as severely as at Ottawa. "I am satisfied,"
says Mr. Bailey, "that as regards soil and climate, this
country is well suited for agricultural purposes." In
March and April yellow butterflies were flying about.
In these months crows were common, and he heard
the rosignol, jay, swamp robin, and Canadian song
sparrow.

At the Height of Land in the Nipissing District the
winters are severe, the summers warm. It is the
great water shedding ridge on whose south side the
streams flow into the lakes, while on the other slope
they pass to the Ottawa.

The Height of Land stretches in a devious course
from north-west to south-east, from the middle of
Lake Tamagamingue until it strikes the St. Lawrence
River near Kingston. It is the central line of a land
of clear streams, and beautiful lakes, with no lack of
fish, game and timber. Proceeding northward the

(*a*) Algoma report.

climate improves owing to diminution in the elevation. The temperature on the coast of James Bay rises in summer to 90°. The shallow water of that bay also exerts a favorable climatic influence. The only place where it is deep is in a channel which passes northward through its centre, elsewhere it is so shallow that the bottom can be touched with an oar from a boat until it passes almost out of sight of the low shore.

The summer sun has great power upon the broad expanse exposed to it. The Albany and Moose Rivers and other affluents entering this bay have also a moderating influence. The mean summer temperature at Moose Factory is about 60°, and the snow fall there is not as heavy as it is south of Lake Nipissing. James Bay is often associated in the popular mind with the Polar regions, yet no part of it is within the Arctic circle, and the latitude of its southern extremity is south of London. Its total area is 500,000 square miles, or half that of the Mediterranean. *(a)*

An indication has now been given of the vast wealth in agriculture, timber, mineral and other resources, held in Ontario's great territory. Expectations of profit from riches so distant and at present

---

(a) The Algoma Report, 37, 38 and 45. For statistics of the weather at Moose Factory for the years 1878 and '79, see report of Canadian Geological Survey for 1879, '80 ; see also, Dr. Bell's observations in subsequent reports of the Survey, as to valuable deposits of coal and other minerals, found on the islands and shores of James Bay.

so difficult of access, as are those of this broad northern expanse, may by many be regarded as sanguine dreams of the visionary. Forty years ago the endeavors of Canadian statesmen to secure the Hudson Bay region from the astute traders who held it was, by the uninformed, spoken of as an attempt to obtain for mere pride of empire, an icy waste, fit only for hunting grounds. Now the buffalo is gone, and those broad hunting grounds form the great western provinces and fertile territory of the Dominion. The praries and hills are crossed by railways, steam vessels ply on all the lakes and rivers, many villages and thousands of happy homesteads deck the landscape,—electric lamps lighten their cities and towns, and their people enjoy the arts of European civilization. Foreign capital is regarding each new discovery with interest, and is ready to develop natural resources.

Children now living will see the day when the people and the interests of James Bay will be referred to as frequently and as familiarly on the streets and in the Exchanges of Toronto and Montreal, as are now those of Lake Michigan or the Georgian Bay. So imperial is our fair province in her proportions, so fitted is her climate for the home of a free, intelligent and industrious race, so all-embracing are her resources, so lavish has kind nature been, that her children, as they regard their bountiful heritage, may well exclaim—

" Far as the heart can wish, the fancy roam,
Survey our empire, and behold our home."

A NATIONAL PARK.—The matter of setting apart a portion of our wild and picturesque northern region, while yet in a state of nature, as a forest reservation and national park, has been mooted and received favorable consideration. Commissioners appointed by the Provincial Government, have recommended the appropriation of a tract of about 750,000 acres, south of the Mattawan River, in the south-easterly part of the Nipissing District.

The place selected will, it is believed, prove well adapted for such Reserve. It is connected with the most romantic period of our provincial history, the time of Champlain, the Hurons and the hardy voyageurs. The Government which, with the friendly co-operation of the State of New York, rescued the beauties of Niagara from vandalism and made there a park which bears the name of Her Majesty the Queen, may well follow up the excellent and popular precedent thus established.

In Quebec the Megantic Fish and Game Club, whose membership embraces many Boston and New York, as well as Montreal, Sherbrooke and Toronto gentlemen, secured a great tract of wild land and water, extending from Lake Megantic over the Boundary Mountains into Maine. This beautiful preserve is guarded by an efficient warden and rangers and abounds with game. It is during the season the resort of many tourists from both lands, who, often accompanied by their families, find here various means of health giving recreation.

The National Park scheme has been well brought before the public in former years by Mr. W. B. Phipps and Mr. A. Kirkwood, officers of the Crown Lands Department. (*a*) In a communication by Mr. Kirkwood, in August, 1886, to the head of the department, he thus refers to the region selected as the source of many waters :

" A glance at the map of the Ottawa and Huron Territory of Ontario shows that the Muskoka River which flows into Lake Huron and the Petewawa, Bonnechere, and Madawaska Rivers, which empty into the Ottawa, have their sources within a very short distance of each other. Island Lake at the head waters of the Muskoka, and Otter Slide Lake at the head of the Petewawa are not half a mile apart, and each is 1,406 feet above the level of the sea.

The head waters of the Muskoka, after flowing in a circui. of 1,000 miles through Lakes Huron, St. Clair, Erie, the Niagara River, Lake Ontario and the River St. Lawrence, meet and commingle in happy harmony with those of the Petewawa, Bonnechere, and Madawaska near the city of Montreal."

Mr. William Houston, late librarian of the Ontario Parliament, spoke of the park scheme in a recent public address, from which the following is quoted :

To one acquainted with the growing craving of Americans, and especially of those who live far to the south of us, for a pleasant "summer resort," the first sight of the Laurentian region, as it was a century ago, would at once suggest that it should be reserved as a continental park. For such a purpose it is absolutely unique, not merely in America, but so far as we know, in the world. It is perfectly salubrious. It affords enough of sporting amusement at all seasons to stimulate to

(*a*) The name proposed is Algonkin Forest and Park. The tract of land selected by the commissioners, contains the following nineteen townships ; Wilkes, Pentland, Boyd Biggar, Osler, Lister, Deacon, Devine, Bishop, Creswick, Anglin, Hunter, McLaughlin, Bower, Dickson, Peck, Canisbay, Sproule and Preston.

physical activity. It contains an endless diversity of scenery. It is easily accessible, or can be made so in every part. There are enough of good farming plots to maintain a constant supply of those animal and vegetable foods, that are too perishable for transport from a distance. Where the country has not been denuded of its evergreen forest covering, the climate surpasses that of any other place in the heat of summer. The United States Government has set apart a national park 400 miles square on the Yellowstone river, but its chief peculiarity is its volcanic character, which is incompatible with that sylvan beauty which forms a more enduring attraction. New York State, seeing with regret the disappearance of the Adirondack forests is endeavoring at great expense to check destruction, and partially restore the primitive condition ; but the Laurentian region far surpasses the Adirondack district, alike in extent and in those physical characteristics which fit for park purposes. Preservation of the forest is not incompatible with the removal of trees that are valuable as the raw material for manufactures, or with the raising and smelting of metalic ores. In view of the possible development in the transmission of electric power, the vast aggregate of water power now useless for any local purpose may yet prove of great economic value, but its continued existence unimpaired, depends absolutely on the preservation and restoration of the forest.

At the present rate of destruction of the pine forests the lumber industry will soon become greatly reduced in extent south of Lake Nipissing, and a once beautiful landscape of rock, wood and water, will be practically a barren wilderness. Along with the progress of settlement, has gone the destruction of game and the exhaustion of fish. It has always been, and will always be, found impossible to prevent settlers from killing game at any season. It is part of their food, and no system of police can ever keep them from appropriating it. All the game destroyed by fall hunters is insignificant in amount compared with what is destroyed by settlers, who kill all the year round. Detecting and punishing contraventions of the game laws by sportsmen will do something to check the waste. Meanwhile, though the " summer resort " idea has been left to spontaneous development it has reached immense proportions. Those waters that are most accessible by rail and steamer, are fringed with summer hotels and summer cottages, and "guiding" sportsmen and other tourists has become the regular calling of a large number of the residents. The remedy is apparent.

The beginning of a more enlightened treatment of this

district was made by the Legislature of the province last year, when it enacted a more stringent game law, based on the report of a commission of experts. A further and still more important step in advance will be taken if the report of the Park Commission should result in the reservation of a large area of land from settlement in the Nipissing district. The site suggested is well fitted for the purpose and object aimed at. Fish are abundant in its lakes and streams ; the locality is the natural home of the moose and the red deer ; smaller game of many varieties, including birds, are more plentiful than almost anywhere else ; and fur-bearing animals of several highly-prized kinds are indigenous. The idea inaugurated by the commission, will, it is hoped, take root and grow rapidly in the public mind.

Reverting to the Georgian Bay and its immediate interests, we find that most of the marketable pine and some of the hemlock and spruce along the sides of the Bay, and for some distance up its tributary rivers, have been stripped, but a great supply remains yet, as has been shewn, in the interior. The roads, cut through the woods, by former lumber men may be found half grown over, and are beautiful pathways, from which glimpses of lakes are seen, and the hunter finds them convenient when seeking his game. Here and there he comes to a beaver meadow, but the busy colony is gone.

In some places, as at the mouth of the Musquash and French rivers, and at the great mills in the North Channel, the round timber is brought to the water's edge, sawed into boards or other lumber, and so prepared for the market. But often all that is seen, as the result of the work of an army of axe-men, is the great raft, covering several acres in extent, tugged along to Bay City, Cheboygan, Saginaw or other

10

Michigan harbours, the logs grinding together and throwing off much bark, which sinks, fouls the nets and drives the fish away.

Among the lumber-men in our northern forests are many citizens of the United States; some estimate their number as high as four thousand. Their families still reside in that country, whose alien laws debar Canadians from such employment there, unless they foreswear allegiance to Britain.

The American companies cutting on the Canadian side, bring their plant and supplies with them, and the wages paid go back to the States. Why do these lumber-men tow the logs to Michigan to be there manufactured, instead of erecting and using mills on our shores for the purpose ?

The answer is, *The McKinley Bill.* That Bill fixes an import duty of two dollars per thousand on Norway pine, and one dollar on white pine lumber. It also provides, that if any country should impose an export duty on logs of any kind, the import duties shall remain as under the former law, at two dollars per thousand. The export duties being removed, it leaves the Georgian Bay manufacturer at a disadvantage, the logs going to Michigan free, and the lumber paying a duty of two dollars on Norway, two on spruce, and one dollar on white pine. The difference more than pays the cost of towing.

This discrimination, of one and two dollars per thousand feet, enables the lumbermen to tow and manufacture in Michigan at a profit.

We found matters of grievance among the fishermen, who complain of the injury done to their industry by the sinking bark, as also by the sawdust and refuse allowed to fall into the water from mills. They desire the initiation by the Dominion of a Canadian policy, which would compel the lumbermen to manufacture into lumber before removal from the shore.

It is doubtless of importance that these matters be arranged, through the general and provincial governments, in a manner that will best conserve the large interests involved.

However interesting such themes may be, it is on other topics that our memories will most kindly dwell as we recall the happy days and nights spent on the "White Squall." We will remember the majesty of forests and granite shores. We will hear the scream of gulls and see the flash of great fish struggling in the nets. We will see in fancy the jolly fishermen steering merrily among the rocks. We will hear their songs and stories, as each sat, with brown, weather-beaten, friendly face, on a pile of nets or on a box in our camp. There still rises to our ears the gay laugh of the Indian boys about the wigwams. We will not forget the beauty displayed in winding, glassy coves among the islands, in flowers and verdure in sunny nooks, the Aurora dancing each clear night in the north, the kindly courtesy of our little company, the chaff of the camp fires and the songs we sung, of which the following is one, composed 'mong the Isles of the Georgian Bay :

'MONG THE ISLES OF THE GEORGIAN BAY.

Some sing old Ocean's praise
Where wild winds the billows raise,
And the whale and the porpoise play,
Some vaunt famed Biscay's Bay ;
And the fair for the South wind sigh.
But give to me that shore,
Where the North star shines most clear,
And our devious course we steer
'Mong the Isles of the Georgian Bay.
      CHORUS—Oh give to me, etc.

And we think, as the "White Squall" glides,
Or we rest on their mossy sides,
What strange tales could these isles unfold
Of the brave red men of old !
The plaintive loon we hear ;
The dappled deer appear
In the glades, as our merry bark flies,
And our devious course we steer
'Mong the Isles of the Georgian Bay.
      Oh give to me, etc.

Of the Genöese Captain, (*a*) in quest
Of new lands in the far sunny West,
Of De. Champlain, with fleur-de-lis spread ;
Of the brave Arctic hero, (*b*) who sped
O'er these waters, pray tell us great Pines,
Ye whose heads the clouds piercing, arise ;
Ye too, surely remember the cries
Of the Mohawk and Huron at strife
'Mong the Isles of the Georgian Bay.
      Oh give to me, etc.

By the Clematis' fairy bower
Blooms the Columbine's purple flower ;
While blue bells gay to the golden rod,
Wild roses to violets nod,
And smile down on the gem-spangled moss,
The brown bee hums : "Your joys I hear,
"And bring sweets for your evening cheer,
"Pure as dew and as amber clear,"
'Mong the Isles of the Georgian Bay.
      Oh give to me, etc.

With shrill scream from the rocks,
Rise the white gulls in flocks,
While far down in the deeps,
With cold eye, the great sturgeon creeps.
In the tangle of vine and dark spruce shade,
Is the bed of the black bear made ;
From the coiled rattle snake,
Manito ! safe us make !
'Mong the Isles of the Georgian Bay.
    Oh give to me, etc.

At eve, with sun-set beams,
La Cloche's gray rock gleams,
With bright spirits from Algic (c) skies,
See, the swift Aurora flies.
O'er the pines the pale moon smiles.
All enwrapped in the beauty of night,
We look on, by the camp-fire's light;
Great Manito seeming near,
'Mong the Isles of the Georgian Bay.
    Oh give to me, etc.

(*a*) Columbus.

(*b*) Sir John Franklin.

(*c*) Algonquin, including Ottawa and Chippewa.

APPENDIX *A* TO CHAPTER V.

TABLE OF INDIANS OF ONTARIO AND QUEBEC, COMPILED FROM THE CENSUS.

ONTARIO.	1867.	1891.
Chippewas and Munceys of the Thames.......	588	637
Moravians of the Thames.................	254	309
Chippewas, Pottawatomies and Ottawas of Walpole Island..........................	748	852
Wyandots of Anderdon....................	71	98
Chippewas of Snake Island................	130	127
Chippewas of Rama......................	265	226
Chippewas of Christian Island.............	186	357
Missisaugas of Rice, Mud, and Scugog Lakes..	282	283
Mohawks of the Bay of Quinté.............	664	1,120
Missisaugas of Alnwick...................	212	243
Ojibways of Sandy Island	174	....
Chippewas of Saugeen....................	280	579
Chippewas of Cape Croker................	352	396
Christian Island Band on Manitoulin Island...	71	. ..
Six Nations of Grand River...............	2,779	3,474
Missisaugas of the Credit.................	204	253
Chippewas of Lake Superior...............	1,263	2,051
Chippewas of Lake Huron.................	1,748	3,177
Manitoulin Island Indians................	1,498	1,915
Golden Lake Indians.....................	164	367
Chippewas of Sarnia.....................	....	479
Pottawatomies of Sarnia.......	....	34
Oneidas of the Thames...................	....	726

QUEBEC.	1867.	1891.
Iroquois of Caughnawaga	1,596	1,798
Iroquois of St. Regis	797	1,218
Lake of Two Mountain Indians	593	375
River Desert Indians	317	455
Abenakis of St. Francis	268	378
Abenakis of Becancour	67	62
Hurons of Lorette	276	301
Alalacites of Viger	170	121
Micmacs of Restigouche	378	471
Micmacs of Mara	113	94
Montagnais of Lower St. Lawrence	1,039	1,701
Scattered Bands	....	1,816

" From the foregoing it will be seen that there has been a considerable increase during the past twenty-five years, and the re-arrangement of the bands has been such that it is not always easy to place the proper figure opposite each band."

A considerable addition should be made to those here classed as Indians in respect of the Metis population in which the red man is often lost in the newer race. Many also of those classed and living as Indians are of mixed blood. The Hurons of Lorette, near Quebec, have less physical trace of the aborigines, as known to Champlain and the Jesuit Fathers, than any other band in Canada. They are shrewd in business, and on a par with the French habitants about them. The half-breed population of the bay and north shore has been already referred to.

APPENDIX *B* SHINGUACOSE.

As the Ottawa warrior has been referred to somewhat fully, it seems but right to recall something of the brave and loyal Chippewa, whose fame was in all the Lake Superior region, second only to that of his predecessor Waub-Ojeeg. Mr. J. G. Kohl, the German traveller and savant, soon after the decease of Shinguacose, in 1858, visited this Indian region and found him celebrated throughout it. He had, with a large party of Canadian Indians, joined the force which attacked and took the Michigan stronghold, on the seventeenth July, 1812. When the mode of attack was considered, Captain Roberts called on the Ojibway Chief, for his advice. He took a night to consider, or as he said, to dream about it. In the morning Shinguacose gave advice which was adopted. The whites, with beating of drums and firing of guns, attacked in front, while the red allies paddled out in canoes, climbed the heights unnoticed, and made an unexpected attack upon the American rear. This filled the enemy with terror; Fort Holmes was soon surrendered. The event was one of much importance. The post was the Gibraltar of North-Western Canada. The command of the upper lakes and the control of the fur trade was secured to Canada. An attempt was made to retake the place two years later, in which Assikinack was concerned as already stated, but Macinac remained a British post and Canadian soldiers held the fort, until given up when peace was declared.

Had Shinguacose been a white man, he would have been decorated and knighted. He had well won his spurs, and his loyalty, as also that of Assikinack, were of manifest service to the Empire. As it was he received a cheferie and a grant of land near Sault Ste. Marie as his reward. He was given several medals for bravery which he never wore, but gave to his young warriors. In the histories of the period, we find the Indian allies massed together, with little regard to individual actions or prowess. The names of minor officers of white blood, are reported for every deed of any note, while the red men are treated but as so many dogs of war.

Shinguacose was son of a Scotch officer by a Chippewa squaw. When a young man, he was taken by his mother to see his father, then serving in the Detroit garrison. The officer gazed with pleasure on the young savage. He was proud of him, and wished to educate and bring him up as a white man. He proposed this, and promised to procure his son a commission in the English service. But no; Shinguacose soon made up his mind; he would not leave his faithful mother, Indian relatives and customs. His father dismissed him with presents, and retained a paternal interest in him until his death. When the war was over he followed the British and came to Garden River, where a pine was erected before his lodge, on which flew the red Union Jack. He was long a leader of his people, and headed several expeditions into the Sioux country from Lake Superior to the Mississippi. He was then a pagan, and full of superstition; in a medicine bag he carried recipes for magic incantations, which he valued most highly. For these he had, at various times, paid in beaver and other skins, what was calculated by Mr. Khol, as amounting to $30,000. But, under the ministrations of Dr. McMurray, he became a Christian, and settled at the Indian village of Riviere au Desert, highly esteemed by his people and the English. As he lay in his last illness, the red folk prepared and put up a second flag-staff before his house, with a new flag upon it; but he died, leaving a worthy family, one of whom, Augustin Shingwauk, gave his name to the Shingwauk Home. It was found that the old chief had, shortly before his death, destroyed all his papers and birch-barks, painted dreams, songs and dances. (*a*)

APPENDIX *C*.

THOMAS GEORGE ANDERSON.

Captain Anderson was one of the most noted and useful officers in the early employ of the Canadian Government. He was well versed in Indian languages and customs, and was the friend of the Assikinacks father and son.

The Ottawa Indian Department states that its records show that Thomas George Anderson was appointed to the position of Indian interpreter, 27th August, 1816, he being then 25 years of age. He served at Drummond Island, and afterwards had his headquarters at Toronto and Cobourg. He retired on ac-

---

(*a*) Kitchi-Gami. By J. G. Kohl, cap. 23. The Canadian Indian, p. 153 and 343.

count of ill-health, in July, 1858, on a good pension. A letter
from him, found in the Department, contains the following :—
"My Dear Sir,—You wish to know when I was appointed to
the Indian Department. In the early part of 1814 I raised a
corps of volunteers, and after the capture of Fort McKay, on
the Mississippi, I remained in command of the post for some
time.

"At the close of the war, I returned to Michillimacinac, in the
commencement of the year 1815. From this I was sent back to
the Mississippi, formally to announce the conclusion to our allies
in that country. In the meantime my commanding officer,
Lieut.-Colonel, now Major-General McDowall, had recommended me for a permanent situation in the Indian Department, and after my return from this duty to Drummond Island,
I received my appointment on the 24th September, 1815, as
Captain in the Department, and have remained in it ever since.

　　　　　　　"I am, dear sir,
　　　　　　　　　"Yours faithfully,
　　　　　　　　　　　　"T. G. ANDERSON.
"To GEORGE VARDEN, ESQ."

The name of Anderson appears in Lossing's History of the
war more than once. On 28th May, 1813, at Sackett's Harbour,
he states that Lieutenant Anderson had forty Caughnawagas,
who were landed at Henderson's Bay, and helped to create a
dread, which ended in a disorganized retreat. He also appeared
at Chrysler's Farm, November 11, 1813, in command of some
Indians.

APPENDIX *D.*

THE ASSIKINACKS.

An American version of the taking of Fort Dearborn is given in Drake's *Indians
of North America*, v. 134.

The signatures of the Indian delegates who presented their
case to the Executive in 1811, are copied from the original, on
fyle at Washington, and kindly given through Mr. R. V. Belt,

Acting Commissioner of Indian Affairs, Department of the Interior, who states: " The treaty of Fort Wayne was sent to the United States Senate, December 22, 1809, by President Madison, with explanatory documents. It is impossible now to determine whether any reference was made in these documents, to the presentation to " Black Partridge" of the medal referred to, as the Capitol and its records were burned and destroyed in 1814. I transmit herewith a copy of the talk or petition of Barstow or Kimi-ne-tega-gan, and of " Black-Bird," or Siginoc, two Ottawa chiefs, signed at Washington, which is the only paper I am able to find that refers in any way to "Black Partridge," or "Black-Bird." The document last referred to ends thus :

As to Francis Assikinack, the following is part of a communication from the Department of Indian Affairs at Ottawa, including a facsimile of his signature.

Francis Assikinack entered the Indian Office, at Cobourg, on the 10th August, 1849, as clerk and interpreter, which position he continued to hold, both there and in the Indian office, Toronto, up to the date of his death, which occurred on the 21st of November, 1863.

The following is an extract from a letter received from **Mr. W. R. Bartlett,** who was in charge of the Indian office, Toronto, reporting the illness of Assikinack :

TORONTO, July 1st, 1863.

"I very much fear the poor fellow will never live to come back. I sincerely trust he may recover, for he will be a great loss to the Department, and especially to this branch of it."

"I attach to this letter an original signature of Francis Assikinack, as follows : "

I have the honor to be, sir,

Your most obedient humble servant,

F. Assikinack

WILLIAM SPRAGGE, ESQ.,
Dy. Supt. Indian Affairs, Quebec.

APPENDIX E.

INDIAN PROPER NAMES AND DO-DAIMS.

The nan es applied to places and persons by the Indians are full of meaning and some knowledge of them is necessary to the under standing of their history. The following, arranged mainly under authority of Mr. J. C Bailey, C.E., are given as representative, and are mostly found in the narrative or on the accompanying map.[*]

It is surprising to see how beautifully the language of the Algonquin tribes is constructed. It has naturally a soft, smooth sound; the letters F, L, Q, R, V and X not being in the alphabet of the Ottawa, O-jib-way or Cree proper. Ideas are expressed in groups and a complicated "word-picture" is formed. The language has been compared to the Greek in its sweetness and in its construction. Many differences of meaning are conveyed by changing or adding terminations. With a few exceptions, all the words contained in this list are in the O-jib-way and the kindred dialects of the Algonquins (O-dush-gwah-gah-meeg), O-to-wah, Po-ta-wah-tah-mee, Me-no-me-ne. The Algonquins occupied mainly the region north of the great lakes from Nova Scotia to the Rocky Mountains, as far as Lake St. John in Quebec and Hudson Bay in Ontario.

Ab bi-tib-be, the half-way place, so called, because midway between Lake Nipissing and Moose Factory on James Bay.

Ah-mik, a beaver,—Ahmik Harbour is Beaver Harbour.

Algonquins or Algonkins, also Alinconquins, Algics and Altenkins, so called by the early French, include the Chippewas, Otchipwais, or Ojibways, Ottawas, Adirondacs, Missisaugas, Micmacs, Abenakis, Delawares, Mohicans and some extinct nations formerly in the New England States, also the Pottawatomies, Blackfeet, Montagnais du Saguenay (Saguenay Mountaineers) and Crees.

---

[*] See also *Indian names of places near the Great Lakes*, by D. H. Kelton, Detroit, 1888; *Meanings of Indian words around Sudbury*, by Dr. Bell, Geological Survey, 1891, Appendix IV., and Dr. A. F. Chamberlain's *Language of the Missisaugas of Scugoy*.

Assikinack, the Black-bird.

Assiniboine-se-be is the Stoney Sioux River and should be As-si-ne-bwaun, Bwaun being a Sioux and assin a stone.

Aurora Borealis, Chibayag ninii-diwag, the dead are dancing.

Bobcaygeon should be O-bob-ka-je-wun and means a narrow place between rocks where the water comes through.

Cesebe Lake should be she-sheeb, which means a duck, or Duck Lake. In the Cree se-seeb is a duck.

Chicago means where skunks are; she-kahg being a skunk, ong or ongk being the dative of location, meaning at or to that place.

Coboconk should be Kah-be-kahnk or Kah-kah-be-kahnk, or Pwah-kah-be-kahnk and means fa'ls over a smooth rock where the water falls straight down and not sloping.

Couchiching is an inlet as at Orillia. Orillia was and is now called by the Indians Me-che-kuh-neeng, which means narrows dividing two lakes; it is also the word for a fence.

The Credit was called from a trading place or store being there where Indians traded and got credit, hence it was called Mah-ze-nah-e-ga-sebe (se-be being a river), Mah-ze-nah-e-gun being a book where their debts were entered.

Etobicoke should be Wah-do-be-kaung, a place where many alder trees grow; Wah-dobe is an alder tree, Wah-do-be-ke a forest of alder trees, and the termination—ong or ing—meaning at, to, in or from such a place—as ne-be, water; ne-beeng, in the water.

Hamilton on Burlington Bay was called De-o-nah-sa-de-o, a Mohawk word which means a shallow place with a sand bar.

Iroquois or Six Nations, the most warlike native race of North America, embrace the Mohawks, Onondagas, Senecas, Oneidas, Cayugas and Tuscaroras. The last named were not in the original confederacy and before they joined it, the *bund* or union was called the Five Nations. In O-jib-way the Mohawks are called Nah-dah-way, or black snakes.

Joseph, Lake, is Kah-wah-sha-gah-mik, or clear water.

Kaka-beka, see Coboconk.

Kaministiquia, at Fort William, should be Kah-me-niss-tah-qui-yah (se-be), and means a river with an island in it.

Keewatin is Ke-way-din, the true pronunciation being nearer the d than the t, and simply means north, both in the Cree and the Ojibway languages. Ke-way-de-ne-nodin is north wind, nodin is wind.

Kingston in Mohawk is Gah-da-o-qui, and Cataraqui is Kah-dah-rock-qui.

Mackinac or Michilimackinack, is derived from Me-zhe-ka, which in O-jib-wa is a turtle, and the O-tah-wah Indians would say me-ke-nang, and in the Cree mees-ke-nauk ; the O-jib-ways would say for a big turtle me-she-ne-mah-ke-naunk, and the people who live at that place me she-ne-mah-ke-ne-goog ; the Indian tradition being that a very large turtle was found there at the time when the Indians were fond of telling these stories around the camp fires to their children and others who believed in such narratives—(ah-duh-so-kaun).

Mahgenetewan is mah-gah-net-te-waung, a long open channel.

Mashquoteh, where the new Upper Canada College is now built, should be Mahsh-ko-da, and means a meadow or a prairie ; also Mash-ko-se-kun, Mah-nahsh-ko-se-waun, etc. ; the accent, as in most of these words, being strong on the last syllable.

Matawan is a Cree word and is Mah-tah-wawn, and means where a river falls into a lake or some place below.

Manitoba may mean several things. Mah-ne-to is a spirit, and in Ojibway Mah-ne-to-wah-pun or bun means a place where there is something supernatural or Mah-ne-to-bi—sitting God, or Mah-ne-to-wah-bah—a spirit in a strait.

Maskinonge is called no doubt from a fish of that kind, and which in Ojibway is mahsh-ke-non-je. Ke-non-je is a common pike, and mahsh is large or strong.

Matchedash should be Matche-dushk, and means a place where there are rushes and drowned land.

Michigan means a big lake, the word being contracted ; Sah-gah-e-gun being lake, and Mishi or Ma-tchau being large. This is about the same in Cree.

Michi-po-coton means a large mushroom.

Milwaukee should be Me-ne-wah-kee, which means good land— Me-no good, and ah-kee land.

Mississippi means simply a big river ; see-be being river, me-sah being large. Hence the Ojibways would say, Me-sah-see-beeng, to, or at that river ; hence the name in Cree Mis-si-se-be.

Missisauga means a river with many mouths.

Missouri, Mishonisibi, river of the big canoe tribe.

Muskeeg. This word so much used on the C. P. R., should be mush-keeg, and simply means a swamp where trees could grow. Mish-gwuh-si, being a softer kind of beaver meadow ; mahs-kaik in Cree.

Mushquash should be Mush-kahs, and means a white stone or quartz.

Nassagaweya should be Na-zhe-sah-ge-way-yong, and means a river with two outlets.

Nipissing means a small lake—ne-beens being the diminutive and ne-beens-ing—meaning to, at, or from the lake.

Nottawasaga is Nah-dah-wa-sah-ge, which means the mouth of the Mohawk River. Nah-dah-wa being a Mohawk, and sah gee mouth of a river. Me sah-sah-ge means the large mouth of a river.

O-me-me means pigeon ; hence O-me-me-se-be—Pigeon River.

Owen Sound is still called by the Indians Ke-che-we-quaid-ong. Ke-che is large and we-quaid is a bay, and the dative termination ong, as already explained, to, or at that place.

Parry Sound is called by the Indians Wah-sah-ko-sing, meaning white all around the shore.

The Sault Ste. Marie is called Pah-wah-teeg, which means falls or rapids.

Pembina is said to be a corruption of the Cree word Ne-pe-me-nah, which means the high bush cranberry. In Ojibway they are called uh-neeb-me-nun. The low bush cranberries growing in the swamps are called mahsh-keeg-me-nun. Nepimina got corrupted into its present shape by Hudson Bay Company employees and coureurs de bois.

Penage, Lake, is Wash-kah-gah-meeng, meaning Crooked Lake. Penage is the French word for a pair of deer's horns.

Penetanguishene is from two words and means the Rolling Sand.

Saguenay is a Cree word and is Sah-ge-ne pe, meaning water going out.

Saugeen means mouth of a river.

Shing-wauk is a pine tree, the diminutive Shingua-cose or Shing-wauk-ons, is a small pine. The township Chinguacousy should be Shing-wauk-ons-e-ka—a pinery or where young pines grow. Holland Landing was called this by the Indians. The "Shing-Wauk Home" at the Sault Ste. Marie being called after the Indian chief of that name who formerly lived at Garden River and who was son of Shingua-cose.

Severn is Wai-nant-keche-aung, and means a river running about in all directions.

Scugog should be Pi-yaug-wash-kew-gaug and means a shallow muddy lake.

Spadina should be Ish-pah-de-nah and means a high hill or rising ground, Ish-pah being high ; Ish-pah-me-gudt, it is high ; Pe-kwah-de-nah, it is hilly ; Ish-pah-be-kah, a high rock.

Sheboygan should be Shah-bo-e-gah-neeng, and means the place where the water can be used right through by a boat or canoe without making a portage (o-ne-gum).

Simcoe, Lake, was called by the Indians ah-shoon-ne-yongk, which name, as tradition says, was the name of a dog that continually went about crying out that name, but was never seen.

Shahwahnegah is a long bay or strait. Shah-wa-yah a long strait or shore.

Saskatchewan should be Ke-sis-kah-je-wun, both in the Ojibway and Cree, and means a rapid current ; Pa-meche-wung being a current of water , Ke-se-je-wun is a swift current. Red River was called by the Indians Mis-ko-se-be, misko being red and se-be a river.

Superior, Lake, is Kit-che-gumme, or big sea.

Thessalon, on the Georgian Bay, should be Ta-suh-nong, and is derived from Ta-sin, a flat point of land jutting out into the lake.

Temiscamingue means deep water, from timi or dimi deep, and gum-me lake or water.

Ta-ma-gamingue—Tamagamimg, means a lake of bays.

Toronto is a Mohawk word and should be De-on-do, meaning trees in the water. There is some doubt about the meaning of this word, as the language of the various bands composing the Mohawks varies in dialect.

Wahnapitae should be Wah-nah-be-da-be, and means a row of teeth in a semi-circular shape.

The river Wisawasa should be We-sah-gah-mah-seeng, meaning rapids or water running towards a lake or some other water.

Wigwam should be we-ge-waum, and is a lodge, bark or otherwise.

Wah-we-a-yah-te-nong is Lake St. Clair, and means a round lake, as Wah-we-a-yah means round.

Washago should be Wah-sha-gum-me and means clear water. Wa-sha means clear ; wah-sha-yah, bright, and wah-sa-yah, light ; gum-me being an affix meaning water or lake.

Wawanosh is Wa-wa-naush, and means sailing well. Wa-wa-ne-well and nah-sheeng, sailing.

Winnipeg is from the Cree ; wini, dirty, and pek, a swamp ; pronounced we-ne-paik.

11

Do-daims. -Each tribe has its crest, totem, or more properly dodèm or do-daim. Bands have also sometimes their particular do-daims, being rudely carved or painted designs. These may be seen on canoes, paddles and other articles. Their most important use was in the execution of documents, such as treaties and deeds.

No trace of the employment of a do-daim by the Assikinacks can be found in the Indian department at Ottawa nor in Washington. The other Ottawa chief who signed with Assikinack the document of October 5, 1811, affixed his proper crest, a grey squirrel, as has been seen. The following are examples of do-daims used by the tribes or bands mentioned, both Algonquin and Iroquois : -

Algonquins,	of Montreal	a Green oak.
Nipissings,	of Two Mountains	a Heron.
Ottawas,	of Ottawa River........	a Grey squirrel.
Tabittikis,	of Lake Temiscamingue..	an Eagle.
Iroquois (Six Nat'ns)	of U. States and Canada.	Wolf, bear, deer, small bear, turtle and snipe.
Hurons,	of Lake Huron	Cord, rock, etc.
Ojibways,	of Lake Superior........	Loon and bear.
Missisauga Riv. Ind.	of St. Clair, Quinté, and formerly also of Toronto	a Crane.
Petuns,	of Georgian and Huron Peninsula	Wolf and stag.

CPSIA information can be obtained
at www.ICGtesting.com
Printed in the USA
LVOW13s0841051217
558693LV00017B/864/P